Poles

IN WISCONSIN

Susan Gibson Mikoś

WISCONSIN HISTORICAL SOCIETY PRESS

Published by the Wisconsin Historical Society Press
Publishers since *1855*

© 2012 by the State Historical Society of Wisconsin

Publication of this book was made possible in part by a grant from the Amy Louise Hunter fellowship fund.

On the front cover: A Polish immigrant stands near a team of horses eating hay in the market square at Stevens Point, 1890. Stevens Point was the main commercial center for surrounding Portage County farming communities. *WHi Image ID 38664*

The excerpt of "Memoir of My Life" (Polish version) by Maciej Wojda is used by permission of the Polish Museum of America in Chicago, Illinois.

Printed in the United States
Designed by Jane Tenenbaum

27 26 25 24 23   3 4 5

Library of Congress Cataloging-in-Publication Data

Mikoś, Susan Gibson.
Poles in Wisconsin / Susan Gibson Mikoś.
p. cm.
Includes bibliographical references and index.
ISBN 978-0-87020-422-7 (pbk. : alk. paper) 1. Polish Americans—Wisconsin—History. 2. Polish Americans—Wisconsin—Social life and customs. 3. Immigrants—Wisconsin—History. I. Title.
F590.P7M55 2012
977.5'0049185   dc23

2011044941

Acknowledgments

This small book on a large subject could not have been written without the groundwork laid by others. Besides the authors listed in the "Selected Bibliography," there are a number of scholars whose research contributed substantially. They include Steven Avella, Dariusz Ciemniewski, Victor Greene, John Gurda, Martin C. Perkins, John Radzilowski, Thaddeus Radzilowski, Helen Stankiewicz Zand, Edmund Zawacki, and many more.

I am indebted to the Independence Public Library, the Milwaukee County Historical Society, the Milwaukee Public Library, the Polish Museum of America, the Polish National Catholic Church Commission on History and Archives, the Portage County Historical Society, the Pulaski Area Historical Society, the Archives Department of the University of Wisconsin–Milwaukee Libraries, the Nelis R. Kampenga Archives of the University of Wisconsin–Stevens Point, and the Wisconsin Historical Society for generously sharing their collections and expertise.

Finally, I wish to thank the Wisconsin Historical Society Press, especially director Kathy Borkowski and editor Sara Phillips for skillfully shepherding this book through the development process.

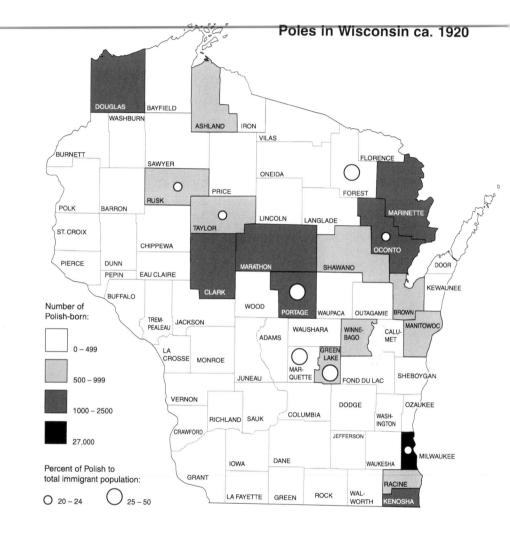

Poles in Wisconsin ca. 1920

Number of
Polish-born:

0 – 499

500 – 999

1000 – 2500

27,000

Percent of Polish to
total immigrant population:

20 – 24   25 – 50

DOUGLAS   BAYFIELD
WASHBURN
BURNETT   ASHLAND   IRON
                                                      VILAS
                SAWYER   FLORENCE
                                        ONEIDA
POLK   BARRON   RUSK   PRICE   FOREST
ST. CROIX   MARINETTE
            CHIPPEWA   TAYLOR   LINCOLN   LANGLADE
PIERCE   DUNN   OCONTO
         PEPIN   EAU CLAIRE   DOOR
              BUFFALO   CLARK   MARATHON   SHAWANO
                                                      KEWAUNEE
         TREM-   JACKSON   WOOD   WAUPACA   OUTAGAMIE   BROWN
         PEALEAU   PORTAGE   MANITOWOC
         LA   WAUSHARA   WINNE-   CALU-
         CROSSE   MONROE   ADAMS   BAGO   MET
                                      GREEN
VERNON   JUNEAU   MAR-   LAKE   SHEBOYGAN
                          QUETTE   FOND DU LAC
                                      DODGE   WASH-   OZAUKEE
         RICHLAND   SAUK   COLUMBIA   INGTON
CRAWFORD   JEFFERSON
                                                      MILWAUKEE
         IOWA   DANE   WAUKESHA
GRANT   RACINE
         LA FAYETTE   GREEN   ROCK   WAL-   KENOSHA
                                      WORTH

FOREWORD

The story of Wisconsin's Poles, like the story of virtually every Badger State ethnic group, is a chronicle of family. The immigrants dreamed and labored collectively in the Old World, and when they chose to leave, they made both the decision and the crossing together. First by the hundreds and then by the thousands, Poles traded the hardships they had known in the heartland of Europe for new lives in the heartland of North America.

All too often, it was an even trade. Whether they were grubbing out stumps to clear fields in the Cutover of northern Wisconsin or keeping up with insatiable machines in industrial centers like Milwaukee, Polish immigrants worked brutally long hours at backbreaking tasks for meager financial rewards. But the newcomers also built communities — communities of remembrance and hope. They were determined to transplant the traditions they had received from long-forgotten ancestors, and they were just as determined to make the sacrifices they considered necessary for the next generation's success.

As one of the half-million Wisconsinites who trace their roots to Poland, I am the grateful beneficiary of those sacrifices. The story of my own family could hardly be more typical. My great-grandparents, Franciszek and Apolonia Gurda, owned a small farm near Sławianowo, a minuscule village in what is now northwestern Poland. When their oldest son, another Franciszek, was threatened with conscription into the German army, they promptly sold their land, their livestock, and most of their possessions to finance the long journey to America. An older brother, Michał Gurda, had already settled in Milwaukee, and in 1889 the state's largest city made room for another branch of my family.

With a handful of exceptions, the Poles came too late to be pioneers. Wisconsin's best agricultural lands were largely taken by the late 1800s, and earlier arrivals had long since determined the economic direction of the state's urban centers. Although farming was all he had ever known, Franciszek Gurda took a job in a blast foundry, and he never rose above the rank of laborer. The work was hard when there was work at all, but his foundry wages were sufficient to buy a tiny cottage on Milwaukee's South Side, within sight of the twin spires of St. Stanislaus Church. It was there that he and Apolonia raised five children to adulthood.

The distance the immigrants traveled can be measured in more than miles. Three generations later, my brothers and I all have master's degrees, live in comfortable homes, and work in professions that our ancestors would consider, by any fair standard of comparison, soft. I'm not sure what Franciszek and Apolonia would make of their descendants — if they recognized us at all — but I can guarantee they would be surprised.

It is my family's odyssey and thousands more like it that Susan Mikoś chronicles on the macro level in *Poles in Wisconsin*. Her account is, I believe, the most comprehensive and even-handed treatment ever published of an ethnic group that has long been one of the state's most important.

Wisconsin was clearly a favored destination for Polish immigrants. Milwaukee became one of the nation's great Polish centers — a development studied in depth by other authors. Mikoś tells the city side of the story, but she balances it with a detailed description of Polish settlements far removed from the densely packed neighborhoods and entry-level factory jobs of southeastern Wisconsin. From Stevens Point and its surrounding farm region to the clusters of settlements north of Green Bay, in Trempealeau County, and in a dozen other locales, Polish immigrants left an enduring mark on the state's landscape.

Whether they settled in the city or in the country, Wisconsin's Poles generally stood out from their neighbors: in their hunger to own land, in their practice of what scholars have termed "additive architecture," in their staunch (but never exclusive) Catholicism, and in their taste for grand houses of worship. Susan Mikoś tells the story of Polish Wisconsin in significant detail, from its folkways to its fraternal groups, and she tells it with a welcome attention to context, both global and local.

The story continues in the twenty-first century, of course, and it continues in directions the immigrants could hardly have imagined. Assimilation has kept pace with social and economic advancement, but for many of us, the old ties still bind. When my relatives gather each Christmas to break the *opłatek* wafer and exchange heartfelt wishes for the new year, when I hear my children sing "Sto Lat" (100 Years) for a great-aunt's birthday, and when I pause to consider the distance we've come, I still feel an overwhelming sense of wonder. After all these generations, the story of Polish Wisconsin remains, at root, a story of family.

— John Gurda

INTRODUCTION

Wisconsin is one of the most Polish states in the nation. For most of the twentieth century, Poles comprised the state's second-largest ethnic group, surpassed only by the Germans. According to the 2000 United States census, Wisconsin has a higher percentage of people claiming Polish ancestry (9.3 percent) than any other state, and it ranks sixth in total numbers. Milwaukee ranks fourth among U.S. cities in the number of residents claiming Polish ancestry, and Portage County, Wisconsin, is home to the largest rural Polish community in the country.

From the time Polish immigrants began to arrive in the mid-1850s, they left an imprint on Wisconsin's landscape. Today, settlements with names like Polonia, Pulaski, Sobieski, Poniatowski, Krakow, and Lublin recall Polish pioneers, while schools, parks, and monuments dedicated to Revolutionary War heroes Thaddeus Kościuszko and Casimir Pułaski remind passers-by of Polish contributions to American history. Scores of churches across the state memorialize the Polish immigrants who carried their faith to Wisconsin. A nineteen-mile section of Highway 66 in Portage County is designated the Polish Heritage Highway. Roadside shrines and crosses like those that marked the traveler's way in Poland still stand along some rural roads in central Wisconsin. In Milwaukee, distinctive "Polish flats" identify the old Polish neighborhoods. One of Milwaukee's Polish neighborhoods — the East Village — is listed in the National Register of Historic Places.

Although the neighboring city of Chicago later surpassed Milwaukee's Polish population, Milwaukee was an early destination of Polish settlers, and Wisconsin figures prominently in the annals of American Polonia (a collective term for people of Polish origin living outside of Poland). Milwaukee's St. Stanislaus congregation was the first urban Polish parish in the United States, and St. Stanislaus also established the second Polish parochial school in the nation. Milwaukee's Kosciuszko Guard, founded in 1874, was the country's first Polish military unit. The first successful Polish-language daily newspaper in the United States, the *Kuryer Polski* (Polish Courier), was published in Milwaukee. Two national Polish fraternal organizations — the Association of Poles in

America and Federation Life Insurance of America — originated in Milwaukee. Beyond Milwaukee, Polonia, Wisconsin, was one of the earliest permanent Polish rural settlements in America. The Felician Sisters were the first Polish order of nuns in the United States when they came to Polonia in 1874 to teach in the parish school. In 1936, the University of Wisconsin in Madison established the nation's first Department of Polish. When Cardinal Karol Wojtyła (the future Pope John Paul II) visited the United States in 1976, he toured Stevens Point, Wisconsin, because of the area's large Polish community and its continuing ties to Poland. More than a century and a half after the first Poles settled in Wisconsin, their legacy endures in the traditions and heritage passed down to subsequent generations.

POLISH ROOTS

Historians date Poland's birth as a nation to 966 AD, when Mieszko I, ruler of a pagan tribe called the Polanie, adopted Christianity in the name of his people. In succeeding centuries, Poland gradually expanded its influence in central Europe. During the reign of Kazimierz the Great (1333–1370), Poland's population grew and its territory more than doubled. After the Lithuanian king Jogaila (Władysław Jagiełło) married Poland's young ruler, Jadwiga, in 1386, the combined Polish-Lithuanian state stretched from the Baltic Sea to the Black Sea and covered one-third of the European continent. When Poland and Lithuania formally united in 1569, the Commonwealth of Poland-Lithuania was the largest nation in Europe and the most powerful state in east-central Europe.

Poland's economy was fueled by massive quantities of grain supplied to western Europe. A powerful class of land-owning nobles controlled the lucrative grain trade and dominated Polish society. Poland had a relatively small middle class of merchants, tradesmen, and professionals. The peasants, at the bottom of the social hierarchy, produced the grain that fed Poland's economy and were by far Poland's largest social class. Although the Polish-Lithuanian Commonwealth was officially Roman Catholic, it embraced a number of religious and ethnic minorities. These included several Protestant sects, Orthodox Christians and Greek Catholics, and a significant Muslim Tatar population. During the fourteenth century, King Kazimierz the Great had granted numerous privileges to Jews, and Poland subsequently became home to the greatest concentration of Jews in the world.

Building on a tradition of religious and political pluralism, Poland developed a form of government that, for the time, was singularly democratic and tolerant of diversity. Poland's king was elected by the nobility, and religious toleration was guaranteed. By the middle of the seventeenth century, however, a combination of internal and external forces had begun to erode the Commonwealth's strength. A rebellion of Ukrainian Cossacks (1648–1654) and a Swedish invasion in 1655 devastated much of the country and reduced Poland's territory by more than a quarter. In 1683 King Jan III Sobieski won a spectacular victory over Turkish forces besieging Vienna. Though hailed as the savior of Christian Europe, he was unable to stem the tide of anarchy at home, and his death in 1696 marked the end of the Commonwealth's proudest period. Weakened by a half century of warfare and internal dissension, Poland, with its quasi-democratic government, was no match for the rising military powers of Russia, Prussia, and Austria, which were ruled by absolute monarchs. In 1772 and again in 1793, Poland's three neighbors conspired to appropriate large chunks of Polish territory, and following a final partition in 1795, Poland ceased to exist as a sovereign nation.

During more than a century of occupation, Prussia and Russia both made concerted efforts to suppress Polish national identity. Prussian Chancellor Bismarck's *Kulturkampf* program, initiated in 1871, imposed restrictions on the Roman Catholic Church and prohibited the use of the Polish language in schools and public life. Russia also restricted the Roman Catholic Church and enforced use of the Russian language. The monarchs of Catholic Austria adopted a more liberal attitude toward their Polish subjects, but the Austrian partition, known as Galicia, was the least industrialized and the poorest of the formerly Polish territories. All three imperial powers subjected Polish men to lengthy terms of compulsory military service.

The Polish gentry instigated several attempts to throw off the foreign rulers but failed to gain widespread support from the peasantry. An uprising that began in Warsaw in November of 1830 was brutally suppressed the following year. An 1846 revolt in the Austrian partition backfired when the peasantry turned against the gentry leaders, burning manors and killing many of the local Polish nobility. The last major

Polish uprising took place in the Russian partition in January 1863 and was put down fifteen months later. In the decades following the partitions, a number of Poles from the intellectual and gentry classes left their homeland, some settling in France or elsewhere in Europe, others bound for the newly formed United States of America. Members of the large and diverse peasant class joined the exodus later. Many found refuge in the United States, including Wisconsin.

FIRST POLES IN AMERICA

Polish people have played a part in American history from the earliest days of European settlement. In 1608, barely a year after the first colonists set foot in Jamestown, Virginia, the supply ship *Mary and Margaret* brought "eight Dutchmen [Germans] and Poles" to help the struggling settlers manufacture glass, pitch, tar, soap ashes, and clapboards for timber-poor England. Captain John Smith and others mentioned the Polish artisans several times in their accounts of the first permanent English colony in North America. Throughout the remainder of the colonial era, small numbers of Poles, mainly skilled workers, landed on American shores.

The American War of Independence attracted a hundred or so freedom-minded Polish soldiers. By far the most prominent were Count Kazimierz (Casimir) Pułaski and Tadeusz (Thaddeus) Kościuszko. Pułaski, a Polish nobleman and cavalry officer, came to be known as the "father of the American cavalry." Mortally wounded in the Battle of Savannah, Pułaski achieved almost mythic status as an American hero. Kościuszko, a military engineer, designed fortifications at Saratoga, West Point, and other sites that proved decisive in the American victory over the British. In 1784 Kościuszko returned to Poland, and ten years later he led a national uprising against occupying Russian forces. Kościuszko fought several victorious battles, but in October of 1794 he was gravely wounded and held prisoner in Russia for two years. After his release, he visited his second homeland, the United States. Before leaving for the last time, he drafted a will in which he directed his friend, Thomas Jefferson, to use the proceeds from the sale of his American property to free and educate enslaved people. During the remainder of his lifetime, Kościuszko was widely revered as a military and humanitarian hero. After his death in Switzerland in 1817, numerous monuments were erected to honor his memory, in Poland, America, and worldwide.

Following the final partition of Poland in 1795, small numbers of Poles, mostly members of the landed gentry class, came to the United States in search of political freedom. After the suppression of the November uprising of 1830, 234 captured insurrectionists were allowed to avoid prison by sailing for New York in 1834. One of these Polish revolutionaries — Count Wincenty (Vincent) Serafin Dziewanowski — made his way to the Wisconsin territory. Dziewanowski had been born in 1804 to a Polish landowning family in the Podolia region, which was then in the Austrian partition and is now part of Ukraine. Captured and imprisoned for his role in the November uprising, he arrived in New York in 1834 with the other insurrectionists. After briefly working various jobs in the northeast, Dziewanowski set out for a promised Polish colony in the Illinois territory. Finding the land already taken, however, he moved on and secured a job as lead smelter for W. S. Hamilton in Galena, Illinois. In 1836 Hamilton sent Dziewanowski to Muscoda, Wisconsin, where he managed a smelting furnace. Dziewanowski bought land six miles east of Muscoda near the present village of Avoca. There he built a log cabin and established the first farm in the valley. The township was named Pulaski, reputedly in honor of Dziewanowski's famous countryman, Casimir Pułaski. Vincent Dziewanowski is the first Pole known to have settled permanently in Wisconsin, but he remained isolated from other Polish immigrants. Though said to be devoted to Poland, Dziewanowski read only English books and newspapers. Raised in the Greek Catholic faith, he became a leader in the Methodist church. When he died in 1883, he was buried in Avoca.

FOR BREAD

By the middle of the nineteenth century, European peasants were on the move. Political and economic reforms had loosened the peasants' traditional bonds to the soil, while the Industrial Revolution created new opportunities for wage employment. After being freed from serfdom, Polish peasants were allowed to own small amounts of land. Their holdings often amounted to no more than a few acres, however, and these were usually divided into a number of narrow strips scattered over the common fields surrounding the village. Successive division of farmsteads through inheritance meant that many farms were too small to sustain a family. The poorest peasants owned no land at all, but worked as tenant farmers on large estates or hired out as laborers. While peasants were freed from the land they had been bound to as serfs, landlords were also released from their reciprocal obligations, which had enabled the peasants to eke out a meager living. Now peasants were forced to pay cash rent instead of providing a specified number of days' labor on the lord's estate. Lacking money, they sought seasonal wage employment in the industrial centers of Prussia and in Russian-occupied Poland. Beginning in the mid-nineteenth century, Polish peasants began to venture across the Atlantic to North and South America. Many set out with the intention of earning enough money to buy or lease land in Poland or to pay off debts, and some returned home after doing so. A larger number, however, stayed and built new lives on this side of the ocean.

Historians divide the forces that motivate people to leave their homelands into push factors, or conditions driving them out of the home country, and pull factors, which draw them to a new land. The main factor pushing Polish peasants out of Europe in the second half of the nineteenth century was extreme poverty caused by a severe shortage of land. Fear of being drafted into the armies of the partitioning powers impelled many young men to flee; political repression, cultural suppression, and religious discrimination also contributed to the exodus from partitioned Poland. Nevertheless, the vast majority of peasants who came to America after the Civil War did so for economic reasons. Hence, this mass migration, which took place principally between 1870 and the beginning of World War I, is often said to have been *za chlebem* — for bread.

Like the push forces driving peasants out of Poland, the pull factors drawing them to America were primarily economic, namely, the availability of inexpensive land in rural areas and relatively well-paid jobs in the cities. Once Polish peasants began emigrating, they wrote letters home to relatives and neighbors. Glowing descriptions of life in America induced family and friends to follow. This set in motion a process known as chain migration, in which a few individuals who had moved from a particular village or region were joined by others from the same area. As

settlements became established, the presence of other Poles, and especially the establishment of Polish Roman Catholic churches, exerted a
further pull on would-be emigrants.

Because the economic conditions that drove Polish emigration developed first in the Prussian empire, the mass exodus from Polish lands
started in the Prussian partition, beginning in the 1850s. Many Poles from
the Prussian partition spoke German as well as Polish, which facilitated
their settlement among Wisconsin's large German population. Wisconsin became an early and popular destination for Poles from the Prussian
partition, chiefly the provinces of Poznań (in German, *Posen*) and West
Prussia, with another distinct group from Silesia. Poles from the Austrian
and Russian partitions joined them later, when emigration from those
areas accelerated. In most other states with substantial Polish populations,
the number of Poles from Russian and Austrian territories soon surpassed
those from Prussia, but in Wisconsin, Poles from the Prussian partition
constituted about eighty percent of the total.

It is hard to determine just how many Poles came to Wisconsin
before the First World War. Neither immigration officials nor the U.S.
Census Bureau were consistent in their recording of nationality groups.
Since Poland did not legally exist as a nation, Poles were often counted
as Russian, Prussian, or Austrian, according to which partition they lived
under. Historians agree that Polish immigrants were significantly under-
represented in official records, but no one can be sure by how much.
In 1900 the Census Bureau estimated that about 31,000 Poles lived in
Wisconsin, while many historians believe the true number was closer to
150,000 and some put it as high as 200,000.

BY LAND AND SEA

Polish peasants setting out for the New World faced a daunting journey.
Most had not traveled more than a few miles from their home villages
before boarding the trains that took them to Bremen or Hamburg, which
were the principal ports of embarkation. Some arrived with tickets in
hand, either sent by a relative in America or purchased from one of the
shipping company agents who fanned out across Polish towns and villages

in search of clients. In the port city, ticket agents besieged those who had not yet booked passage. While waiting for their ships to depart, would-be emigrants spent their small savings on food and lodging in overcrowded waterfront rooming houses. Once on board, most were consigned to the least expensive "steerage" quarters, a cavernous space in the ship's hold located near the steering apparatus. Passengers were packed together, with scarcely enough room for their bedding and a few personal belongings. The shipping companies provided rudimentary meals, but most travelers brought dry bread and other staples to supplement the meager galley rations dished up from a common kettle. Diseases spread rapidly in the cramped quarters, and deaths aboard ship were common. By sailing ship, the transatlantic crossing took from six to eight weeks. The advent of steam power in the 1870s cut the journey to about two weeks and lowered the cost of passage.

After a long and often harrowing voyage, the immigrants arrived in New York or another port, such as Philadelphia or Baltimore. Many then boarded trains that took them to upstate New York, New England, Pennsylvania, or the "Northwest," as the Midwest was then known. An early route to the Midwest led from the port of Quebec via the Great Lakes to Chicago, Michigan, and Wisconsin. Some of the newcomers went to join friends or relatives who had already settled in a particular locality. Others were drawn by advertisements in Polish-language newspapers to seek their fortunes in one of the numerous Polish colonies promoted by land developers in Wisconsin and other western states. Most headed first to a big city, where they hoped to find industrial jobs that paid enough money so they could save for property of their own. Wherever they chose to go, Polish settlers sought community with fellow Poles, preferably from the same home region.

POLES IN A NEW LAND

Crossing the ocean to start a new life in a strange land, Polish peasants found security and fellowship with other Poles. In the cities, where industrial jobs attracted large numbers of Polish immigrants, they clustered together in distinct neighborhoods and joined parishes comprised mostly of Polish people. In rural areas, whole communities formed where nearly all of the inhabitants were Polish. The process of chain migration often led to clusters of residents who came from the same region, or even the same village, in Poland.

Once they arrived, however, Polish immigrants faced a new set of social conditions. In Poland, most peasants lived in close-knit villages, with the houses clustered together and long, narrow fields dispersed across the surrounding landscape. One family's land holdings might consist of several widely scattered strips, perhaps adding up to only a few acres. The houses, with their outbuildings behind, stood cheek by jowl, sometimes along a single street, sometimes on several streets, and other times grouped around a green space or pond. In rural Wisconsin, on the other hand, each family lived on a separate farmstead, which often encompassed forty or more acres and isolated them from their neighbors. Deprived of the day-to-day interaction that formed the fabric of Old World village life, Polish settlers in Wisconsin found new ways of building community through religious and social activities. Neighbors gathered in church on Sundays and holidays, as well as for special occasions like weddings and christenings. The local saloon took the place of the Polish village tavern as a place to gather and catch up on the latest news. Organized dances and picnics provided opportunities to socialize with neighbors.

Farm work also brought people together. Both men and women took part in a variety of cooperative work groups that included threshing crews and feather-stripping parties. Threshing was a major activity involving both men and women. Men did most of the heavy work, while women prepared huge quantities of hearty food to fuel the workers. During threshing season, crews moved from one farm to another, the men sleeping in the barn, taking their meals at the farmhouse, and working from sunup to sundown. In winter, women gathered at one another's houses to "strip" goose feathers for use in pillows and eiderdowns. They sang songs and told stories while they worked, and they often shared a meal afterward.

In Poland, every member of the family, from the youngest to the oldest, was expected to contribute his or her labor to the household economy. Polish immigrants, both urban and rural, enjoyed a reputation for hard work. On the farm, the customary division of labor was similar to that in Poland, with the men doing most of the heavy work, such as plowing and operating farm machinery, while the women planted and dug potatoes. Everyone helped with the grain harvest. When it came to live-stock, the men usually worked with the horses while their wives milked the cows, fed the pigs, and tended the poultry. In typical Polish families, the husband and wife shared in both the work and the decision making. Children were given work to do from an early age.

Polish farmers were, from necessity, jacks-of-all-trades. In addition to plowing and planting, they often built their own houses and farm build-ings, fashioned tools, and repaired equipment. During the winter months, many Polish farmers went to work in sawmills or logging camps to earn much-needed cash. While the men were away, their wives took care of the farms and livestock.

Young men and women often spent some time away from the farm earning money before settling down to married life. Young men worked as hired laborers on other farms, or moved to a city to work in a factory. Even if they intended to return and take over the family farm, they needed money with which to buy out the other siblings' rights. Young women were less likely to hire themselves out, but they, too, sometimes worked on another farm, performing such tasks as digging potatoes. Some worked as maids in urban households. It was taken for granted that all family members worked for the whole family, and most sons or daugh-ters who worked away from home contributed to the family income until they were married.

CHURCH AND SCHOOL

The overwhelming majority of Polish peasants who came to Wisconsin in the nineteenth century were followers of the Roman Catholic faith. The first Polish arrivals in a given locality usually worshiped for a time with other Catholics, most often Irish or Germans. However, even though many Polish immigrants spoke German, they preferred to hear sermons in their native language and wanted to observe familiar holiday celebrations. To that end, wherever a significant number of Poles settled, they almost invariably founded a Polish parish.

In Poland, village life had revolved around the church. In Wisconsin, the Polish parish became the center of the Polish community. Among neighbors who might hail from different, sometimes widely separated, regions in Poland, the church was a unifying element. It not only nurtured the Roman Catholic faith but also supported the use of the Polish language and fostered adherence to traditional customs. Once established, a Polish parish acted as a powerful magnet, drawing more settlers to the area. The expansion of one parish often led to the formation of daughter parishes. As a result, the course of Polish settlement in Wisconsin can largely be traced through the history of Polish churches.

The establishment of Polish parishes required Polish-speaking priests. Church officials responded to the exodus of peasants from Poland by recruiting missionary clerics to minister to Polish souls in the Wisconsin wilderness. Probably the first Polish priest in Wisconsin was Father Jan Polak, although information about him is scant. He was active in the Stevens Point area in the 1850s and may have been instrumental in drawing the first Polish settlers to Portage County. He also served in Milwaukee, and is buried there in the priests' section of St. Adalbert's Cemetery. In 1866 a Polish missionary order, the Congregation of the Resurrectionists of Our Lord Jesus Christ — founded in Paris after the failed Polish uprising of 1830 — began educating priests in Rome for assignments in the United States and Canada. The Resurrectionists and other religious orders sent many Polish priests to the United States, including Wisconsin. Together with a cadre of secular clergy, they worked tirelessly to serve a growing number of Polish churches.

With almost every new Polish enclave in Wisconsin, another parish would soon spring up. According to some counts, there were more than seventy predominantly Polish parishes by 1908, and in 1937, more than one hundred. As the face that the Polish community presented to the outside world, an imposing church was both a symbol of devotion and a source of pride. Poor Polish immigrants built magnificent churches, even at the cost of substantial personal sacrifice. A typical congregation began with a modest log or frame edifice and built larger structures as its population increased, until the size and grandeur of the church dwarfed the surrounding parishioners' homes. Some critics railed against the extravagance, but Polish parishioners, frugal in general, rarely balked at expending meager resources on an elaborate church. Splendid churches proclaimed the Polish presence in the new land.

Living in the shadows of their churches, Polish immigrants identified strongly with their parishes. In rural settings, the church usually coincided with the community, or at least the Polish part of it. In urban environments, the parish was synonymous with the neighborhood. A person would say he was from "St. Josaphat's" or "St. Adalbert's," meaning that he belonged to that parish and lived within its boundaries. The parish became a community unto itself, spawning a variety of voluntary associations that substituted for the informal network of extended family and neighbors in a Polish village. Benefit societies, parish support groups, and other organizations provided an essential safety net that aided their members in case of sickness and death. Parish societies also sponsored numerous social events, such as picnics and dances. Churches served as venues for performances by community theatrical groups and singing societies. Parish-sponsored literary societies and clubs sustained the community's cultural and patriotic spirit.

Churches also took on the role of educating Polish children. In partitioned Poland, government-run schools had been alien institutions associated with oppressive foreign powers. Furthermore, education was of little practical value in maintaining a viable farm, which was the peasant's measure of success. Polish immigrants also faced immediate practical concerns that sometimes took precedence over education. In rural areas, Polish immigrants needed their children to work on the farms, while urban laborers depended on the extra income a working child could contribute to the household. It is not surprising, then, that many Polish immigrants viewed schooling — especially state-sponsored schooling — with some ambivalence. Polish parishes, however, particularly in the urban center of Milwaukee, placed great importance on the education of children. Nearly every Polish parish had its own elementary school, and most parents enrolled their children in it. Polish parishioners saw schools as the best means of passing on the Catholic faith and Polish identity to future generations, and they took great pride in having their own schools. An estimated two-thirds of all Polish children attended parish schools, which not only taught the "three Rs" but also strove to maintain use of the Polish language, inculcate traditional values, and instill patriotism.

In the earliest years, Polish parishes employed laypersons, often the church organist, to teach the small numbers of children who were able to attend school. As the immigrant population swelled, a larger pool of teachers was needed. Soon, religious sisterhoods were mobilized to take responsibility for the education of Polish children. These included the Polish Felician Sisters, the School Sisters of Notre Dame (a German teaching order with many Polish sisters), and the Sisters of St. Joseph (a Polish order founded in Stevens Point).

RELIGIOUS DIVERSITY

Poland in its prime had been a multiethnic and multireligious nation, incorporating Roman Catholic, Eastern Orthodox, Greek Catholic, Jewish, Protestant, and even Muslim minorities within its borders. Although the vast majority of Polish immigrants before World War I were Roman Catholic, some Protestant Poles and Polish Jews also came to Wisconsin, as did a small number of Greek Catholics. Most of the Protestant Poles belonged to separatist groups that had originated in Polish territories during and after the Reformation; very few Roman Catholic Poles converted to Protestantism after settling in Wisconsin.

Improbably, the tiny community of Pound in Marinette County became a center of Polish Baptists in America. The settlement consisted mainly of Germanized Polish Baptists who had colonized a small area of Ukraine and later emigrated to Wisconsin. In 1889 German and Polish Baptists in Pound organized a congregation, putting up a church the following year. As more immigrants arrived, the building became too small, and the congregation divided in 1899. The German members moved to a new building and the Poles kept the old church, which they called First Baptist Church. The American Baptist Home Mission Society asked the Polish-born pastor of a missionary church in Detroit, Carl Strzelec, to visit Pound every two months. In 1901 a second Polish Baptist church was formed in Pound, and in 1905, Reverend Strzelec was appointed pastor of both congregations. In 1912 Strzelec was sent to Milwaukee, where he organized Christ Polish Baptist congregation in 1913 and built a church at Nineteenth and Rogers Streets in 1914.

Polish Methodists also established a small congregation in Milwaukee. Rev. Fredrick Rosinski organized St. Peter's Polish Methodist Episcopal Church on Milwaukee's South Side in 1910, and two years later the congregation built a small frame church at Seventh and Hayes Avenues (now 2401 South Twelfth Street). Rev. Stanley Maslowski was brought from Scranton, Pennsylvania, to serve as pastor in 1923, and by 1927 the congregation had grown to embrace 115 members.

The Polish-Lithuanian Commonwealth had been home to the largest concentration of Jews in the world, and after the partitions, Jews from former Polish lands also came to Wisconsin. About 1902 or 1904, Milwaukee Jews from Polish territory founded a congregation called Agudas Achim Anshe Polen (Brotherly Association of Men of Poland), with just over a dozen members. They held services in a small house on Sixth and Cherry Streets, which was then the center of the Orthodox Jewish neighborhood. Although the congregation was the smallest in Milwaukee, it grew rapidly in the second decade of the twentieth century. In 1917 the congregation purchased a large home at 670 Eleventh Street, which they converted into a synagogue. In 1920 they bought land on College Avenue in Cudahy and established an Orthodox cemetery. The congregation was formally incorporated in March of 1920, and by 1924 its membership had grown to 140. In subsequent years, many members moved away, especially to the northwest side of town. After World War II, a large number of Polish Jews came to Milwaukee as refugees from war-torn Europe. They included Rabbi Israel Feldman, who was sponsored by Congregation Agudas Achim and offered the position of spiritual leader. Many of the refugees from Poland joined his congregation, and the synagogue again became too small. A new one was built at 5820 West Burleigh Street and was dedicated in 1955.

Most Polish Jews settled in cities and established themselves as shopkeepers and tradesmen. Others, however, made their way to Wisconsin's small towns and rural areas. For instance, nineteen-year-old Charles Segall came to the United States in 1911 and, after a few years in Milwaukee, moved to the Pulaski area in 1916. He traveled from one farm to another selling fabrics, needles, and thread. In 1917 Segall opened his first store in Pulaski. He soon opened another store and finally established a department store, where he accepted chickens, eggs, hides, and rags in payment for merchandise. He was known as a generous benefactor to needy individuals and to the Pulaski community, including the Franciscan monastery.

Polish Catholics in America had always chafed under German and Irish domination of the church hierarchy. Dissident Polish Catholics broke away and established independent parishes as early as 1873 in Polonia, Wisconsin, and later in Chicago, Detroit, and Buffalo. A more significant break occurred in Scranton, Pennsylvania, in 1897, when a young Polish priest, Franciszek Hodur, left the Roman Catholic Church and formed the Polish National Catholic Church (PNCC). The PNCC retained many of the central tenets of Roman Catholicism, but rejected the pope's authority and allowed clergy to marry. More importantly, the National Church used Polish in the Mass rather than Latin, vested control of church property in the individual congregations, and gave the laity a voice in the selection of priests and bishops. These practices addressed many of the grievances Poles harbored toward the Roman Catholic hierarchy. Catholics forming independent parishes elsewhere in the country began aligning themselves with the Polish National Church, which elected Father Hodur bishop in 1904.

It was some years before the schism reached Wisconsin. An energetic PNCC priest, the Reverend Francis Bonczak arrived in Milwaukee in March 1914 and quickly established a following. An organizational meeting took place on May 18. The new parish, called Holy Name of Jesus, purchased two lots at Sixth and Hayes Avenues (now South Eleventh Street and West Hayes Avenue), and held services in the basement until the church proper was completed in 1917. The church council sent Reverend Bonczak to Poland in 1922. He was consecrated bishop for Poland in 1924 but returned to Milwaukee in 1929 and resumed his post as pastor of Holy Name. Polish National Catholic parishes were also established in West Allis and South Milwaukee, as well as in a dozen other Wisconsin communities: Lublin, Mosinee, Pulaski, Cudahy, Beaver, Willard-Conrath, Reid, Armstrong Creek, South Fork-Hawkins, Radisson, Kenosha, and Alpha.

POLES TO WISCONSIN

For Polish peasants, land was livelihood. A wealthy farmer was one who owned land. A peasant without his own land, or whose holdings were too small, was condemned to poverty. Some Polish peasants came to America in order to buy farms or increase their holdings in Poland. Others dreamed of owning land in the United States. Arriving without money, however, most new immigrants first sought paying jobs in industrial areas. The majority ended up staying in cities, but a significant minority later moved to rural areas and took up the agricultural existence they had left behind in Poland. This was especially true in Wisconsin. Nationwide, only about 10 percent of Polish immigrants were farmers, but the proportion was higher in the Midwest and highest of all in Wisconsin, where as many as 30 percent of Polish immigrants earned a living from farming.

By the end of the 1850s, southeastern Wisconsin's most desirable agricultural land had been taken. Central, northern, and western Wisconsin still had abundant tracts of inexpensive land; however, most of it had been stripped of its commercially valuable timber. This less-desirable property was marketed to land-hungry immigrants who were willing to take on the backbreaking work of clearing the stumps and brush to create farmland. Years later, others marveled at the capacity of Poles to cultivate land that many found too daunting. In 1905 an appraiser for the estate of Joseph Wronski, which included property in Hofa Park, wrote to the deceased's lawyer:

> I could not find a buyer for Wronski's land. As to the quality of the land and improvements there is about 10 acres cleared and a small log house built ready for use and the land is low and well covered with pine Stumps. If you can get a Polish buyer he won't give a cent for the work that will be required to clear the Stumps and as to the real value of the land I would not pay over 15 dollars per acre but if you can find a Polish buyer you may do better.

Driven by a strong desire to own land, Poles were ready to invest both money and labor to create productive farms. Contemporary observers like Albert Hart Sanford agreed that the Poles had "opened to cultivation areas that would not have been touched by other nationalities."

RURAL POLISH SETTLEMENTS

Although the Milwaukee area's burgeoning industries attracted the largest number of Polish immigrants, Poles fanned out across other parts of Wisconsin as well. As the historian Father Wacław (Wenceslaus) Kruszka wrote, "Here in Wisconsin, just as in the entire United States, it is difficult to count all of the places where there are Poles. It is easier to answer the question of where they are not than it is to answer where they are."

Three principal clusters of Polish rural settlement developed: one in central Wisconsin, straddling Portage County and southeastern Marathon County; one in Trempealeau County in the western part of the state; and another in the northeastern counties of Brown, Shawano, and Oconto.

PORTAGE COUNTY

In 1857 Michael Koziczkowski and his family of nine arrived in the Portage County town of Stevens Point. Koziczkowski came from the Kartuzy district in the Kaszuby region of West Prussia. The Koziczkowskis were soon joined by the families of Adam Klesmit, John Zynda, and Joseph Platta, also from Kartuzy. In 1858 all four families bought land northeast of Stevens Point in the township of Sharon. Koziczkowski continued to write home, and immigrants from the Kaszuby region streamed into Sharon and the neighboring town of Hull. By 1863 there were about thirty Polish families in the area. Their settlement, first called Poland Corner (now Ellis), was the first rural Polish settlement in Wisconsin and one of the first in the country, after Panna Maria, Texas, settled in 1854, and Parisville, Michigan, settled about 1856.

At first, the Polish immigrants worshiped with Irish and German Catholics at St. Martin's Church under Polish priest Father Jan Polak. Tensions soon developed with the other parishioners, however. Desiring their own church, the Poles established a new congregation, St. Joseph's, at Poland Corner in the town of Ellis in 1864. Father Bonaventure Buczyński, a Franciscan missionary, was appointed pastor, and a church was built in 1865. Unfortunately, three saloons located near the church regularly disrupted services. In 1870 a young priest named Józef (Joseph) Dąbrowski took over the parish. As a mathematics student at the University of Warsaw, Dąbrowski had joined the 1863 insurrection against the Russians. Facing arrest, he made his way to Rome, where he enrolled in the Collegium Polonicum, which had just been founded to educate young Poles for the priesthood, under the Congregation of the Resurrectionists. Shortly after his ordination, Dąbrowski met Joseph Melcher, the bishop of Green Bay, Wisconsin, who was in Rome to recruit missionary priests for the rapidly growing Polish population of his diocese. Bishop Melcher offered Father Dąbrowski a position in Wisconsin. Father Dąbrowski spent several months at the seminary in St. Francis, Wisconsin, and in the spring of 1870, he took charge of the small Polish mission in Portage County, about ten miles west of Stevens Point.

Unable to persuade Poland Corner's saloons to close during Mass,

Father Dąbrowski enlisted his parishioners' help to dismantle the wooden church, and moved it a mile and a half east. The church was renamed the Annunciation of the Blessed Virgin, which was later changed to Sacred Heart. The new location became the nucleus of a Polish settlement known as Polonia, which in time grew to be the center of the largest rural Polish community in the United States.

Recognizing the importance of education, Father Dąbrowski had started a one-room school almost immediately after arriving at Poland Corner. In 1874 he arranged to bring five sisters from the Congregation of St. Felix of Cantalicio, Third Order of St. Francis (Felician Sisters) from Kraków, Poland, to teach in the parish school. With limited access to textbooks, Father Dąbrowski also established a small print shop, where he produced schoolbooks and religious materials.

After the move, tensions between the saloonkeepers at Poland Corner and the Polonia congregation persisted. Rather than follow Father Dąbrowski, the saloonkeepers and others established an independent Polish parish at Ellis. In March of 1875, fire destroyed the rectory at Polonia. No sooner was it rebuilt than it burned again, this time together with the church. Arson was suspected. Father Dąbrowski rebuilt the rectory once again and replaced the wooden church with a massive stone structure. He also built a new school and convent for the Sisters. Under the Felicians' management, Sacred Heart School grew rapidly. The Sisters also established an orphanage and soon expanded their mission to other Midwestern communities. When the Felician Sisters decided to transfer their motherhouse to Detroit in 1882, Father Dąbrowski moved with them.

As Poles continued to pour into Portage County, additional Polish parishes were established. These included St. Casimir's in Hull (1871), St. Peter's in Stevens Point (1876), St. Michael's in Junction City (1881), St. Bartholomew's in Mill Creek (1883), Our Lady of Mt. Carmel in Fancher (1884), St. Adalbert's in Alban (1894), St. Bronislava's in Plover (1896), St. John the Baptist in Belmont (1896), and Immaculate Conception of the Blessed Virgin Mary in Torun (1897). By the turn of the century, Poles accounted for as much as a third of the population in Portage County, and many Portage County communities were overwhelmingly Polish.

The Polish settlement in Portage County crossed the county line into southeastern Marathon County. In the village of Bevent, Poles dedicated

St. Ladislaus Church in 1883. Across this part of Marathon and Portage Counties, roadside shrines and crosses similar to those that traditionally marked the traveler's way in Poland can still be seen. Roadside shrines and crosses were erected at crossroads and along the highways of many areas where Poles settled in the rural Midwest, but those of Portage and southeastern Marathon County are notable for their number. In Poland, roadside shrines took a variety of forms, ranging from miniature wooden chapels hung on trees to substantial walk-in structures. In Wisconsin, the most common surviving type is a tall, square brick pillar known as a "column shrine." The upper part of the pillar contains an open space with arched glass windows on three sides, covered by a roof. Behind the windows were placed wood or plaster figures of the Virgin Mary, Jesus, or a saint. Even more numerous than brick shrines were tall wooden crosses, usually with a disproportionately small *corpus* of Christ protected by a curved metal roof.

TREMPEALEAU COUNTY

The little community of Pine Creek in Trempealeau County was settled by another group of Kaszubes who crossed the Mississippi River from Winona, Minnesota, in the winter of 1862–1863. This makes Pine Creek arguably the second-oldest rural Polish colony in Wisconsin, after Polonia. Resident Bohemians and Poles organized St. Wenceslaus parish in 1864. Over time, the Polish population came to dominate and the name of the parish was changed to Sacred Heart and St. Wenceslaus. The state line had little meaning for the Polish residents of Pine Creek, who conducted most of their business affairs across the river in Winona, Minnesota.

A larger number of Trempealeau County's Polish settlers came from two neighboring villages in Upper Silesia — Popielów and Siołkowice. The first Silesian families came to Trempealeau County in 1863, after living for seven years in New Lisbon, Wisconsin. Albert Bautch's family bought land in the Town of Arcadia, while the Lawrence Bautch and Peter Sura families settled in the adjacent Town of Burnside, near present day Independence. In response to their letters home, more Silesians soon joined them. The Poles organized SS Peter and Paul parish in Independence about 1869. Parishioners held services in the home of Peter Sura, just outside the village, until a frame church was completed in 1875. By 1881 there were 150 families in the congregation. Immigration continued to augment the population through the turn of the century. A new and much larger church was built in 1896, and a 1908 addition made SS Peter and Paul the largest church in the diocese of La Crosse. By 1917 the parish had 425 families and more than two thousand individual members.

Another Silesian settlement sprang up in the village of North Creek, five miles northeast of Arcadia. In the spring of 1875, residents founded St. Michael's parish. At first the parish was a mission of Pine Creek. By 1910 it had 120 families, including some who lived in Arcadia. In 1909 the school burned down, and some of the parishioners wanted to move the church to Arcadia. Those who lived in North Creek opposed the move, and the parish split. In 1910 a new Polish church, St. Stanislaus, was organized in Arcadia. Without the leadership of a pastor, the parishioners raised funds and built a brick veneer church, which was dedicated by the bishop of La Crosse in 1911. The pastor from North Creek came to conduct services every other Sunday. In 1912 St. Stanislaus built a rectory and acquired a resident priest. Two years later, the parish added a combined convent and two-room school, engaging two Sisters of St. Joseph from Stevens Point as teachers. In 1925 the school was modernized and became a four-room school to accommodate the growing enrollment. A new convent was also constructed for the sisters, whose number had by then increased to five. In 1942 the church burned down after being struck by lightning. A new and much larger structure, of Romanesque design, was built in its place and was dedicated in 1948.

By 1912 there were four Polish churches and parochial schools in Trempealeau County — at Independence, North Creek, Arcadia, and Pine Creek. The greatest number of Poles lived around Independence, where the largest church was located. The Polish population in Trempealeau County was about thirty-seven hundred, which constituted approximately seventeen percent of the total. In some locales, the percentage of Poles was even higher. Most of them were farmers. Living among the Poles were a few Bohemian families. Writing in 1912, John Kulig noted that the Bohemians had all learned to speak Polish, attended Polish churches, sent their children to Polish schools, and "to all intents and purposes have practically become Polish themselves."

NORTHEASTERN WISCONSIN

A third major center of rural Polish settlement developed in the northeastern counties of Brown, Oconto, and Shawano. Northwest of Green

Bay, an extensive Polish colony developed as the result of specific re-cruitment efforts by an enterprising land agent, J. J. Hof, who brought more than one thousand Polish families to the area between 1877 and 1900. Hof's settlement included the communities of Pulaski, Sobieski, Krakow, Kosciuszko, and Hofa Park in Oconto and Shawano Counties.

J. J. Hof (originally Jan or Johann Hofhaug) was born in 1842 in Domaas, Norway. Little is known about him until 1875, when he began his career as a land agent for the General Land Office Company in Milwaukee, owned by William, John, and Ephraim Mariner. Hof at first sold land in and around Seymour, in Outagamie County, to Norwegian settlers. This enterprise failed, however, as the Norwegians soon left the area. In the summer of 1877, newspaper ads and broadsides began to target Polish families in Milwaukee, urging them to settle on the cutover land near the future village of Hofa Park in the Shawano County town of Maple Grove. Hof promised that this was the beginning of his plan to settle many Poles in the area and that if he was successful, more Polish "colonies" would follow.

In September 1877 the first Polish settlers moved from Milwaukee to the northwestern section of Maple Grove. They were Valentine Peplin-ski, Valentine Zygmanski, Michael Lepak, and Frank Lepak, originally from the province of West Prussia. To attract Polish settlers, Hof em-ployed a Polish-speaking secretary, as well as Polish interpreters and agents. Beginning in 1881, he launched a massive advertising campaign aimed at Polish immigrants in the United States. In lots of five thousand at a time, he printed land maps and pamphlets in the Polish language, describing in glowing terms the opportunities for Polish agricultural com-munities that his lands offered. He also distributed thousands of letters listing the names of Polish settlers already occupying land in his "colonies." In these letters, the settlers praised the conditions of life on the farms they had purchased from Hof. In addition, Hof advertised ex-tensively in Polish newspapers all over the country, especially Milwaukee, Chicago, and cities in New York and Pennsylvania. Hof's advertising campaign was concentrated in the years 1885 to 1900, although he con-tinued to advertise his Polish settlements until 1905.

Following his initial success in settling four Polish families in Hofa Park in 1877, Hof established additional Polish "colonies" in the area: Pulaski (1883), Sobieski (1892), Kosciuszko (1895), and Krakow (1897). Pulaski became the largest and most successful of Hof's Polish settlements, while Kosciuszko never did develop into a thriving community. Between 1877 and 1900, the population of Hof's Polish communities grew from four families to 650, and Poles owned nearly one hundred sixty thousand acres of farmland.

Hof realized how important the Catholic faith was to prospective Polish settlers, and one of the chief inducements he used to attract Poles was religious, by incorporating sketches of comely churches in his advertising materials. The advertisements neglected to mention that the settlers had to build the churches themselves. Nevertheless, Hof donated the land and most of the timber, and within five to ten years of initial settlement, each of Hof's Polish communities had its own church: Hofa Park (1883), Pulaski (1887), Sobieski (1897), and Krakow (1903). In 1887 Hof donated 120 acres of land in Pulaski to the Polish Franciscan Fathers. Under the leadership of Brother Augustine Zeytz, the Franciscans established a church and monastery that served all the Polish settlements in the area. After 1887 Hof featured the Franciscan monastery prominently in his advertising materials, using it to attract additional Polish settlers to the area.

Many settlers were disillusioned when they saw the land Hof had sold them. Though advertised as prime farmland, most of it was full of stumps, hardwoods, and cedars. Instead of the fertile fields depicted in Hof's advertising circulars, would-be farmers encountered dense forests and brush, deep swamps, and poor soil. Instead of abandoning the enterprise, however, the Poles dug in to clear the land and begin farming.

Lacking a church of their own, for the first three years after 1877 the Polish settlers of Hofa Park traveled to Seymour to attend services at St. John the Baptist Church, whose parishioners were mostly German. Since most of the early Hofa Park settlers were from the German partition of Poland and understood the language, this was a natural choice. The round trip normally took three days and was made only once a month. On other Sundays, the settlers gathered in a particular home to recite the rosary, litany, and other prayers. From 1880 to 1883 the priest from St. John the Baptist Church traveled to Hofa Park once a month to hold services in someone's home or in Hof's temporary land office. Finally, in 1883, having attained the requisite number of sixty families, the parishioners received permission from Bishop Krautbauer in Green Bay to build a church. J. J. Hof donated the land and the timber, Bishop Krautbauer contributed sixty dollars, and the parishioners provided the

labor. The small log church of St. Stanislaus was completed in the spring
of 1883.

The presence of a church in Hofa Park spurred additional Polish
settlement, and by the end of 1884, the parish numbered 104 families. At
first, it was served by part-time priests from Seymour and Menasha. In
1886 Hof began collecting money to build a larger church, which was
completed in 1888. About the same time, a Franciscan monastery and
church were built in Pulaski. The two parishes shared a pastor until 1892,
when St. Stanislaus parish in Hofa Park was able to build a rectory in
which to house its own priest, Father Stanislaus Jeka, a Franciscan who
had formerly served the parish at Polonia, Wisconsin.

Despite their initial disappointment, the Polish colonists viewed Hof
as more than a land salesman. Hof offered settlers a full complement of
essential services, including mortgages to finance the purchase, home
building, and plowing. He sold the land at ten to fifteen dollars an acre
and was willing to wait beyond the term of payment of principal, sometimes even canceling the interest. He donated land and materials for the
building of churches and helped to finance the construction of roads. He
even held picnics so the settlers could become acquainted with one
another.

Less than twenty years after the first Polish settlers had arrived, Hofa
Park was a thriving farm community. In 1894 Father Joseph J. Fox
reported on his observations of the Polish settlements at Hofa Park and
Pulaski: "The colonists all came from Poland [originally] and the result of
their labor can now be seen in the fact that they are all happy and prosperous people. Their small farms are in good condition, their homes are
tidy and neat, and an air of health and prosperity permeates everything."

Although J. J. Hof was married twice, he died childless. For more
than thirty years, his life revolved almost entirely around his Polish
"colonies." Hof learned to speak Polish, at least to a limited extent, and
when St. John Cantius parish was organized in Sobieski in 1897, Hof —
a Lutheran — became a dues-paying member. Six months before his
death, Hof converted to the Catholic faith. He died on December 10,
1910, at the age of sixty-eight and was buried alongside his Polish
"colonists" in the cemetery of St. John Cantius in Sobieski.

Other communities also grew during this time, though the process of
founding churches did not always go smoothly. A Polish church had been
established in Green Bay as early as 1874, but barely two months after its

1875 blessing as St. Stanislaus Church, the property was sold at a sheriff's sale. A month later, it was bought back by the Diocese of Green Bay, which in 1880 sold the building to a fledgling Polish parish in nearby Pine Grove. The Pine Grove parishioners dismantled the church building and moved it to a farm south of Pine Grove, where they had purchased three acres for a nominal sum. However, because of a dispute over the location, the building materials lay untouched for more than two years. The parishioners finally agreed on another site, and Holy Trinity Church was dedicated on December 9, 1883.

In the neighboring town of Eaton, SS Cyril and Methodius Church had been erected in the unincorporated community of Poland in 1881. Newly ordained Father Peter Chowaniec came to serve as pastor in 1883, and within a short time he was also ministering to the mission church at Pine Grove. Father Chowaniec organized public processions in which the faithful carried religious banners and sang hymns, as in Polish villages. He also erected a number of roadside crosses in the area around Pine Grove. In 1892 the church received its first resident pastor. In 1898 the pastor of the Pine Grove church organized a Polish parish in Green Bay. At first a mission of Pine Grove, the Green Bay church later spawned its own parish, St. Mary of the Angels.

OTHER POLISH SETTLEMENTS

Besides the major rural settlements in central, western, and northeastern Wisconsin, Poles also settled numerous other communities scattered across the state. Small groups and individual Poles intermingled with other ethnic groups in many areas. Significant enclaves of Polish settlement developed in Manitowoc County, in the Northwoods, and along the southwestern shore of Lake Superior.

MANITOWOC COUNTY

Polish immigrants established a significant presence in Manitowoc County beginning in the early 1860s. In 1868 they formed a Polish church named St. Casimir's in the settlement at Northeim and established a school several years later. About the same time, Poles began moving into the city of Manitowoc, where they found work in the rapidly growing industrial plants. Polish settlement was concentrated in an area known as Polish Hill, in the southwest part of the city. As in other urban Polish communities, nearly every household had a large backyard vegetable garden. Many families kept chickens, and some even had a pig or cow. In the early years of the twentieth century, fifty to a hundred women could be seen carrying dinner buckets with hot midday meals from Polish Hill to their husbands in Manitowoc's various manufacturing plants.

As in so many Polish immigrant communities, the Manitowoc Poles first belonged to a German-Irish parish. From 1868 to 1870, the Polish priest from St. Casimir's in Northeim visited them once a month to conduct services in Polish. In 1870 the Manitowoc Poles organized a parish of their own, which they named St. Mary's Catholic Church of the Immaculate Conception. They built a small frame church and, in 1874, purchased a larger frame building from the German Lutherans, which they moved to Polish Hill. Four years later, the parish began construction of a new church, but lack of funds delayed its completion until 1899.

In 1889, Father Zdzisław Łuczycki, who had come from Poland, built St. Mary's home for the aged and orphans of his parish. He brought Polish Felician Sisters to run the home, which became an important benevolent institution. In 1934 the orphans were sent to other Catholic institutions, but St. Mary's continued to serve as a home for the aged.

A number of Poles also settled in the village of Two Rivers. In 1889 Poles established the parish of Sacred Heart and built a small brick church that served until 1899, when a larger church was constructed and the former church was converted to a school. The 1895 Wisconsin State Census recorded 365 Polish families in Manitowoc's Seventh Ward, 263 in Two Rivers, and a total of 507 in other parts of the county.

THE CUTOVER

By the turn of the twentieth century, Wisconsin's northern counties, collectively known as the Cutover, had given up nearly all their supply of virgin white pine to commercial logging enterprises. As it consumed the forests, commercial logging left behind a devastated landscape littered with enormous stumps, small trees, and dense brush. Once the timber was exhausted, lumber companies were eager to dispose of the land, rather than continue to pay taxes on it. Sometimes they simply sold it directly to would-be settlers, but more often, middlemen and land agents bought up large tracts for resale, or several lumber companies formed a consortium to dispose of unwanted land.

Enterprising land agents lured would-be farmers from far-off cities by touting the region's agricultural potential. Their efforts were encouraged by the University of Wisconsin's College of Agriculture and abetted by local and state government officials eager to find new uses for northern Wisconsin. Since Yankee and other native-born Americans were thought to lack the fortitude required to break the stony, stump-ridden land, advertising campaigns targeted land-hungry immigrants in Wisconsin and neighboring states. Exploiting the tendency for immigrants to cluster in ethnic enclaves, Cutover land agents aimed their sales pitches at specific ethnic groups. Most of the purchasers had already worked in the United States for an average of ten years and saved up modest amounts of money with which to buy land. Many of them were Polish.

One of the earliest efforts to colonize Cutover lands with Polish pioneers took place in northwestern Marathon County. In 1880 a Milwaukee land agent named Frederick Rietbrock established the town of Rietbrock and began selling land to Polish laborers. The Poles concentrated in a settlement called Poniatowski, named after Stanisław August Poniatowski, the last king of Poland. In 1882 Polish Catholics formed Holy Family parish in Poniatowski and built their own church six years later.

Another land-selling scheme was conceived by Hieronymus Zech, a Chilton businessman who in 1896 purchased the holdings of the Butler-Mueller Lumber Co. in Marinette County. At Ellis Junction — renamed Crivitz a year later — Zech built houses, warehouses, stores, schools, and roads, and even provided funds for a church. Through advertisements in Polish-language newspapers, as well as agents in Milwaukee and Chicago, Zech aggressively pursued Polish immigrants. If a prospective purchaser was short of cash, Zech was only too willing to accept his city home in exchange for a piece of Cutover land. Between 1896 and 1899 Zech sold twenty thousand acres in Marinette County, much of it to Poles.

Zech's success inspired 150 Polish families in Chicago to organize their own corporation in 1899. They named it the Polish Industrial Company and bought up most of Zech's Crivitz holdings. They had grand plans to settle as many as two hundred families and rename the town Polska (Poland). Optimism ran high. The Marinette *Eagle* gushed, "This is without any question one of the best deals that has ever been made in Marinette county, as far as the benefit to the county is concerned. The Polish people are the most prosperous class of people to locate on land, as they are hard workers, very saving, and make every cent count." Polish settlers poured in. In May of 1899 a huge crowd attended the dedication of St. Mary's Church in Crivitz. Bishop Messmer of Green Bay presided. A special train brought visitors from Chicago and Milwaukee. Milwaukee dignitaries included Comptroller Czerwinski, two newspaper editors, and the Kosciuszko Guards. The colony's success was short-lived, however. On August 9, 1900, fire destroyed ten houses and a large part of the lumber mill. The company tried to rebuild but was forced to declare bankruptcy. Nevertheless, Zech and the Polish Industrial Company had brought thousands of Polish settlers to Marinette County, and their success in colonizing Cutover lands encouraged others.

One of the largest Cutover colonization efforts was that of Eau Claire land developer Benjamin Faast. In 1907 Faast formed the Ben F. Faast Land and Colonization Co. and purchased nearly thirty thousand acres in Rusk County around Conrath and Sheldon and south of Weyerhauser. Focusing on immigrant groups in the Chicago area, Faast's Wisconsin Colonization Company offered dreams of idyllic rural life in Sawyer County, revolving around the planned community of Ojibwa on the banks of the Chippewa River. Of the various nationalities that settled in and around Ojibwa, Poles were the largest group.

Several Polish entrepreneurs targeted their own countrymen in Cutover development schemes. In the northern Clark County area of Thorp and Withee, Milwaukee land agents Felix Piotrowicz and Edward Słupecki drew Polish and Lithuanian families from around the United States with their promise to establish a Polish colony known as Poznań, or Posen. Settlers began arriving in 1889, and by 1891 they dedicated a small wooden church in the village of Posen, two miles east of Thorp. Milwaukee politician and land agent Theodore Rudziński bought twelve thousand acres south of Crivitz in 1897 and settled a number of Polish families in the town of Beaver. In 1910 the Worzalla brothers of Stevens Point (publishers of the Polish-language newspapers *Rolnik* and *Gwiazda Polarna*) bought more than twenty-six thousand acres in Marathon County for a Polish community named Pelplin (later changed to Peplin). They mailed attractive brochures printed in Polish and placed advertisements in Polish newspapers across the United States.

Like their countrymen in other parts of the state, the Polish immigrants who settled Wisconsin's Cutover established their own churches wherever possible. Communities too small to support a resident priest were served by visiting Polish priests from other parishes, but they often went to great lengths to be able to worship in their own language. In 1915 Rev. Wacław Kruszka, the energetic pastor of St. Adalbert parish in Milwaukee, helped to establish a Polish church in the small Rusk County town of South Forks, five miles north of the village of Hawkins. Father Kruszka obtained a thousand dollars from the Catholic Extension Society of Chicago, while the parishioners raised the rest of the money to build the church, in addition to providing the labor. They named it Our Lady of Częstochowa, after Poland's most revered icon of the Virgin Mary and the shrine devoted to it, regarded by the devout as the most sacred place in Poland.

In the northeast corner of Forest County, the town of Armstrong Creek became home to a small but strongly Polish settlement. Because of its remote location, the area developed relatively late. In 1914 the residents founded St. Stanislaus Kostka parish. On the secular side, they organized a branch of the Polish National Alliance in 1919. From the 1930s until 1972, there was also a Polish National Catholic church in Armstrong Creek.

The Poles and other immigrants who settled Wisconsin's Cutover region faced a daunting task. Before farming could begin, the land had to be cleared of stumps and brush. This was a laborious and expensive process. Even though various kinds of mechanical stump-pullers were devised, these were costly and of limited help. Dynamite came into general use only after World War I, and it, too, was expensive. Struggling to overcome the stumps, stones, and brush, Polish settlers fought to fulfill the dream of owning their own farms. In the end, however, the short growing season, uneven soil quality, and distance from markets doomed many of them to failure. During the winter months, farmers were fortunate if they found work in factories or sawmills, leaving the women and children at home to tend the livestock. In 1920, a devastating drop in farm prices exacerbated the hardships of an already precarious existence.

On the eve of the Great Depression, the Wisconsin Colonization Company declared bankruptcy. At the same time, active attempts to promote agricultural development of the Cutover region as a whole came to an end. State officials began to encourage reforestation of the denuded land, and the region reinvented itself as a vacation destination. Some of the would-be farmers abandoned their hard-won land, while others found new work in the outdoor recreation industry, and a few persevered. A liberal scattering of Polish (or formerly Polish) churches across the region testifies to the numbers of Polish immigrants who took part in the bold endeavor to turn Wisconsin's northern forests into fields.

LAKE SUPERIOR

Polish settlers began moving into Wisconsin's northernmost reaches in the early 1880s. Since the area was not conducive to farming, the Poles came to work in the lumber camps and sawmills, build the railroads, and toil on the docks. The two largest Polish settlements were in the cities of Superior and Ashland, with smaller clusters in Butternut, Washburn, and Cable. At first, Polish Catholics had to be content with occasional visits from Polish priests who traveled, often long distances, from other parts of Wisconsin and even from other states. In 1899 Ashland's Poles founded the first Polish parish in Wisconsin's far north — Holy Family Catholic Congregation. The parishioners opened a school in 1901 and completed the church in 1902. In 1901 Poles in the larger city of Superior formed St. Stanislaus parish, bought an old Congregational church, and moved it to their own site. In 1902 another group of about fifty Polish families in the eastern part of Superior began looking for their own Polish parish, and in 1909 the old St. Francis Church became St. Adalbert's Polish parish church.

FARM, FOOD, AND FAMILY

Wherever they settled in the world, Polish farmers adapted their agricultural practices to the prevailing environmental conditions. In Wisconsin, Poles followed the same trends as other farmers, growing wheat in the 1870s and 1880s and later shifting to dairy farming, or, in the sandy soils of central Wisconsin, potato culture. In the early years, Polish immigrants tended to grow more rye than other ethnic groups, but they also cultivated oats, barley, corn, and beets. In addition, they raised a variety of livestock, including cattle, swine, sheep, and poultry. Conservative in their agricultural practices, Polish farmers relied more on hand labor than machinery. Initially, the Poles depended more heavily on oxen than other ethnic groups. Oxen were cheaper and easier to feed than horses, and they were especially useful for breaking soil and pulling stumps. Once the major clearing had been done, however, Polish farmers increasingly used horses for routine plowing and harvesting.

Family members provided most of the labor for clearing and tilling Wisconsin's stump-covered and often rocky soil. In contrast to their Yankee and Irish counterparts, but like Germans and Norwegians, Polish farm women worked long hours in the fields, alongside the men. Reluctant to hire farmhands, Polish immigrants were willing to endure personal hardship in order to improve their farms. Only after they had cleared their debts did Polish farmers begin to purchase machinery and nonessential items for the home. This ability to sacrifice temporary comfort enabled many Polish immigrants to turn marginal land into productive and even prosperous farms.

The monotonous diet many Polish immigrants were accustomed to from the old country improved substantially in America. Meat and white bread, which had been comparative luxuries in Poland, were readily available in Wisconsin. As in Poland, pork was the preferred meat; beef, rarely eaten in Poland, was the second most popular meat in Wisconsin. Eggs and dairy products were important sources of protein in both Poland and Wisconsin. Soups were an essential element of the Polish American diet, as they had been in Poland. *Czarnina*, a sweet-and-sour soup made with duck or pig blood, was a particular favorite among Poles from the Poznań region; *barszcz* (sour beet soup), cabbage soup, chicken broth with dumplings, pea soup, barley soup, mushroom soup, and sorrel soup were but a few of the nearly endless variety of soups. As in Poland, cabbage and potatoes figured prominently in the diet of Wisconsin Poles. Sauerkraut with potato dumplings was an everyday main course and something to fall back on during hard times. In Portage County at the end of the nineteenth century, Polish people baked bread from rye flour and sometimes added potatoes, as in Poland. Fine wheat flour, which had been a delicacy in Poland, was used both for bread and for various kinds of noodles and dumplings. Potatoes with sour milk — a staple of the Polish peasant diet — was also a common dish among the early Polish settlers of Portage County. For festive occasions, Polish homemakers in Wisconsin prepared more elaborate foods, such as pierogi (half-moon-shaped dumplings filled with meat, cheese, mushrooms, sauerkraut, or blueberries), *zrazy* (beef roll-ups), *gołąbki* (stuffed cabbage rolls), and various types of kielbasa (sausage).

Used to producing food for their own consumption, Polish peasants were notoriously averse to spending money on food. Even in urban settings, they maintained vegetable gardens and often kept cows, pigs, and poultry. On farms, animals were raised to supply meat and dairy products, and vegetable gardens were a necessity. Cabbage was one of the most common vegetables grown, since it could be kept over the winter, pickled and packed in fifty-gallon barrels. Root vegetables like rutabagas, carrots, onions, and beets were also popular because they could be stored in cellars. Herbs were grown both for cooking and for medicinal purposes. Portage County resident Michael Lisz recalled that his grandmother was "a great one for herbs." She had a "beautiful herb garden" with about thirty different herbs planted in rows forty or forty-five feet long. Some of the herbs were used for Polish sausage, while others were crushed and sold to drugstores.

The Polish immigrants' strong attachment to family entailed a complicated system of family obligations that often extended back to Poland, with immigrants sending money home to support the family farm. As in Poland, the farm in Wisconsin was considered to belong to the entire family. Fathers expected one of their sons — often, but not necessarily, the youngest — to take over responsibility for running the farm at some point. Even children who left the farm to work in the cities or on farms of their own retained an interest in the family farm, returning home frequently and contributing money, as well as labor, to maintain it. As in Europe, when the farm passed undivided to one child, the inheritor typically bought out the rights of the other children, usually through cash payments.

Like other central European and Scandinavian immigrants, Polish farmers often provided for their retirement by transferring the land to the next generation before they died. In return for title to the land, one child agreed to take care of the parents as long as they lived and then give them a proper funeral. This practice not only provided a means of support in old age but also helped to keep the farm in the family and allowed for a smooth transition from one generation to the next. Legal documents called bonds of support spelled out the type of housing arrangements and food that were to be provided. For example, in 1894 Stanisław

Pisczek of Maple Grove in Shawano County signed a lifetime support agreement with his father, Anton Pisczek, promising to furnish him annually with twenty-five bushels of wheat, twelve bushels of potatoes, two hundred pounds of pork, the use of one cow, seven dollars in cash, and "all necessary stove wood fitted for use." Stanislaw further promised to "have all the clothes properly mended and washed, also to provide a suitable room for the said Anton to live in." Agreements such as these were common through the 1930s. Some agreements included the use of a horse and buggy for a specified number of days, or transportation to church on Sundays.

MAKING A HOME

While brick was used for building houses in some regions of Poland, especially in the Prussian partition, wood was more common in other regions, and it was far more plentiful in Wisconsin. Many Polish immigrants had grown up in log homes and were skilled at log construction. Unlike the typical American "log cabin," derived from Scandinavia, Polish log construction utilized tight-fitting squared timbers with finely dovetailed corners. The first log homes built by Polish immigrants in rural Wisconsin were one story high with steeply pitched roofs and ample attics. They generally had only one or two rooms and a few small windows. Thatched roofs made from rye straw were used on some of the earliest houses and barns, but these were soon supplanted by wood shingles.

Although they drew on familiar building methods at first, Polish immigrants were quick to adopt new construction techniques. For example, a unique type of building called stovewood construction was unknown in Poland but was readily adopted by Poles and other immigrant groups in the upper Midwest and Canada, probably because it was inexpensive and easy to put up. Stovewood construction utilized eighteen-inch logs that were stacked as if for a woodpile and set in mortar. The technique was commonly used for utilitarian structures in rural areas, where nearby sawmills produced an abundant supply of the requisite log segments. The Kruza House, an early immigrant home that was moved from Hofa

Park to Old World Wisconsin, an outdoor museum in Eagle, is a well-preserved example of stovewood construction. The Kruza House also reflects an ancient European practice, known in Poland, of combining house and barn under one roof, with separate doors to each area. August and Barbara Kruza, an elderly Polish couple, lived in one side of the house and kept chickens in the other.

Like other pioneers, early Polish immigrants commonly lived in one- or two-room log houses. By the turn of the century, however, Polish farmers were putting up frame houses instead of log buildings. Balloon construction made it possible to construct wood-frame houses quickly and cheaply. Some land developers offered ready-made cottages in a choice of two or three different versions. Once they became established and began to prosper, Polish farmers built large Victorian farmhouses that were indistinguishable on the outside from the homes of other well-to-do farmers.

When it came to home furnishings, Polish immigrants were limited in what they could bring from Poland. Anna Maciej's family, from Popielów in Upper Silesia, carried more goods than most. When this family left its comfortable brick home in Poland, "their load was packed not only with axes and grub hooks and spades, but also with a lovely china vase decorated with its bouquet of painted roses and urn-like handles, with a dozen of gaily decorated plates and cups and saucers, as well as bowls and baskets, shawls, and beads and holy pictures," Anna told an interviewer in the 1940s. Poles were known to bring musical instruments, spinning wheels, flower and vegetable seeds, holy pictures, and crosses across the ocean. They sometimes asked relatives coming later to bring particularly treasured items, such as a religious icon, song books, a favorite variety of tobacco, or a scarf.

Religious items from the old country were greatly prized. Most often immigrants wanted to have a picture of the Virgin Mary or another religious icon from their home region. They often tucked treasured devotional items, such as a crucifix, prayer book, rosary, or holy picture, into their baggage, and what they didn't bring with them, they bought in Wisconsin. The Stevens Point newspaper, *Rolnik* (The Farmer), had its own stationery and religious goods store, which advertised a wide variety of items. On April 7, 1899, for example, there were "holy pictures, imported from Europe, colored and monochrome, in various sizes and for low prices," as well as picture frames, prayer books, scapulars with both Polish and English inscriptions, rosaries, crosses, holy water fonts, candles, and candlesticks.

Furniture in rural Polish homes was limited to a few basic items, often including the trunk that had carried the immigrants' worldly possessions from Poland. Like the dowry chests that were a prominent piece of household furniture in Poland, immigrants' trunks were often used to store the family's bed linens and best clothing. Peter Kush of Armstrong Creek, Wisconsin, noted that, besides the holy pictures, the only object from Poland that he remembered in his boyhood home was the round-top trunk his mother had brought over. According to Mary Kowal and Zuzanna Kulig of Independence, their family's first tables were the trunks brought from Upper Silesia. Albert John Bautch's parents brought two trunks when they came to Wisconsin from Upper Silesia in 1854, and one was still in the family in 1946. Polish immigrants who traveled with little else in their trunks almost invariably brought bedding from home. Once the original bedding from Poland was no longer serviceable or sufficient, immigrants used feathers and down from their geese and ducks to make new Polish-style eiderdowns and large feather pillows.

In the earliest years, some furniture was homemade. Mrs. Kulig recalled that her first log home had stumps with boards stretched across for benches and straw pallets on the floor for beds. Later, her husband bought two chairs in Trempealeau, and they had a bed and table built by an itinerant cabinetmaker. Even though little furniture was brought from Poland, European-style bedding and religious objects combined to give the earliest immigrant homes a distinctly Polish flavor. Many houses had a home altar, as in Poland, and there was usually a small holy water font inside the door.

Household furniture was basic, generally consisting of one or two beds, one or two tables, three or four chairs, one or two stoves, and perhaps a cupboard. Curtains were a luxury for most rural Polish families. As in Poland, paper curtains with cut-out designs were sometimes substituted for fabric or lace. In Trempealeau County, paper curtains were still being used as late as 1946. Carpets were a rarity. Some of the early settlers of Portage County continued the Polish custom of sprinkling brightly colored sands on the floor to create festive designs for Easter and other holidays.

Not all of the household arts practiced in Poland survived the transplantation to America, but many women were proficient in embroidery and crocheting. Another popular craft involved fashioning crepe paper flowers, which were placed around holy pictures to add color for holiday celebrations. Stationery and religious-goods stores listed "paper for flowers" in their newspaper advertisements.

DRESS AND PERSONAL APPEARANCE

Writer, publisher, and public official William George Bruce remembered seeing newly arrived Polish immigrants on the streets of Milwaukee in the 1870s: "The young women with their head covering of colored and white bandannas, and the older women in their small lace caps, proved a picturesque innovation on our conceptions of modern wearing apparel." As late as the 1930s, Bruce noted:

> Frequently, even now on a Sunday morning, elderly Polish women may be seen going to church, wearing the bulging homemade skirts and the pretty white lace caps of a former day. At the same time, the younger Polish-American women and girls of the day cannot, either by their dress or manner, be distinguished from their sisters of other nationalities in other sections of the city.

While still in Poland, prospective emigrants were advised by friends and relatives in the United States to leave their old country clothing at home, lest they be laughed at. Male immigrants abandoned their high boots, loose trousers, and long shirts in favor of American shoes, shirts, and pants. Women, especially older women, were more conservative. Instead of weaving their own cloth, as in Poland, they fashioned clothes out of American factory-made fabric, but often according to Old World styles. While their husbands and daughters adopted American cuts, Polish immigrant women often clung to their full skirts, long aprons, head kerchiefs, and shawls. Even younger immigrant women wore kerchiefs on their heads for everyday occasions. Many older women from the Prussian partition favored white tulle bonnets, with a ruffle framing the face and wide bonnet strings tied under the chin.

As in Poland, it was a matter of self-respect to have good clothes to wear to church. Men usually bought their suits from a tailor, but women made clothes for themselves and their children, often following the same simple patterns. Some of them also kept a few sheep to provide wool, which they spun at home and then knit into stockings, hats, and mittens. Many women continued to knit woolen stockings for their families even after factory-made stockings became available.

HOLIDAYS AND FAMILY CELEBRATIONS

The Polish year revolved around the church calendar, and Polish immigrants continued to celebrate most of the major religious holidays much as they had in Poland. Some of the minor holidays, however, as well as observances that were not part of the church calendar, fell out of practice in the New World setting.

In many Polish communities, Advent was observed as a period of fasting, abstinence, and preparation for the twelve-day Christmas holiday. The most important part of the celebration was Christmas Eve, which was observed with a traditional *Wigilia* (vigil) supper. The meal was replete with symbolism. Before sitting down, all the family members shared a special wafer, called *opłatek*, and exchanged wishes. The *Wigilia* supper was a meatless meal, but it featured a rich array of dishes, including fish, various kinds of pierogi, mushroom or beet soup, sauerkraut, and noodles or dumplings. For dessert, there might be dried fruit compote and poppyseed cake. After supper, the family would gather around a Christmas tree, decorated with homemade ornaments, to sing traditional Polish carols. At midnight, parishioners gathered in church to celebrate Midnight Mass.

Felix Swiecichowski, born in 1914, remembered celebrating Christmas Eve in Hofa Park. His family always had a tree with candles on it. After sharing the *opłatek* and exchanging good wishes, his family enjoyed a traditional Christmas Eve supper consisting of three courses, including herring and a cream soup. There was not much emphasis on gifts, but as a little boy, he might get something he needed, like a new pair of pants. The family all attended Midnight Mass. In many Polish communities, the Feast of the Epiphany, on January 6, was celebrated as in Poland: chalk, gold, and myrrh were blessed in church and "K+M+B" (for the three kings, Kacper, Melchior, and Baltazar, separated by crosses) was written with blessed chalk on the frame over the door, where it remained for the rest of the year.

The Carnival season — the six-week period between Christmas and Lent — was a time of gaiety, when parties and weddings were held in many Polish American communities. Filled doughnuts, called *pączki*, were traditionally served during the week before Ash Wednesday. In most Polish communities, Lent was observed much as in Poland. No parties or weddings were held, dress was somber, and no meat was eaten. The week before Easter was spent in preparation. The house was thoroughly cleaned, and the Easter fare was prepared. The day before Easter, in some parishes, the priest went to people's homes to bless the Easter food; in larger parishes, the food was brought to the church in large baskets or hampers to be blessed. Easter began with a Resurrection Mass, held at dawn. Following this, people returned to their homes for the Easter meal (*Święcone*) — a cold but sumptuous feast consisting of the food that had been prepared earlier in the week: boiled eggs, ham, sausage, horseradish, bread, and salt. The meal began with the family sharing a blessed egg and exchanging good wishes. Easter Monday was also a holiday. It was devoted to various kinds of merrymaking, known as *dyngus*, *śmigus*, or *śmigus-dyngus*. In many communities, boys continued the Polish custom of dousing girls with water or hitting them with switches, which the girls reciprocated by soaking the boys in return.

Other church holidays included Ascension Day, *Boże Ciało* (Corpus Christi), and the Feast of the Assumption. People went to church in the morning and then visited relatives in the afternoon. On Corpus Christi Day in many Polish communities, outdoor altars were set up and trimmed with branches or saplings. After celebrating Mass, the congregation formed a procession, stopping at each of the altars. The Feast of the Assumption (August 15), known in Poland as *Matka Boska Zielna* (Our Lady of the Herbs) was observed in some Polish communities in the early years. On this day, the women took bouquets of field flowers and herbs to church to be blessed. The blessed bouquets were taken home and displayed in a place devoted to other blessed objects, usually beneath the principal holy picture.

Besides the church holidays, family weddings and christenings were occasions for social gatherings. A new baby was usually baptized seven to ten days after birth. Following the ceremony, the new parents invited neighbors and relatives to their home for a celebration. In Hofa Park, a pig or calf would be slaughtered, along with some ducks or geese. Beer flowed and a band played. Children were usually named for a saint — often, but not necessarily, the saint on whose day they were born. Birthdays were not celebrated by Polish immigrants; as in Poland, "name days" (i.e., the feast day of a person's patron saint) were observed instead.

Dancing was the most popular form of entertainment for any celebration, both in the United States and in Poland. In central Wisconsin, the band was usually a string ensemble consisting of several violins and a bass fiddle, with a clarinet or cornet added. Later, after about 1910, the concertina came to prominence. Dances were held in barns at first, and later in public buildings or dance halls. Traditional Polish dances like the *oberek*, *kujawiak* and *mazurka* were popular and were later joined by the homegrown American, multiethnic polka.

The polka originated as a Bohemian (Czech) folk dance that became popular in ballrooms and on stages across Europe in the 1840s. German and Central European immigrants brought it to America with other folk and popular dances. After a time, the polka fad died out in Europe, but polka acquired a new life in America, where it merged with the traditional dance music of various European groups and developed a variety of ethnic and regional styles. The origin of the name "polka" has been the subject of much speculation. In the Czech and Polish languages, "Polka" refers to a Polish woman; it has also been suggested that the term is a corruption of a Czech expression meaning "half step." Later, however, the word "polka" became a generic designation for a variety of musical styles that developed in America, based on European folk music. Wisconsin's Polish bands incorporated polka numbers into their repertoire of traditional and international tunes. Polka music was also popular among other ethnic groups, but a distinctive "Polish" style emerged in the 1920s and reached a peak of popularity in the 1930s. Encouraged by a voracious recording industry, an increasingly professional cadre of Polish American musicians borrowed melodies from Polish folk songs and incorporated Polish lyrics into their singing. Even though polka music evolved on American soil, its popularity among Polish Americans led many to regard it as a musical expression of Polish heritage.

Weddings were the most important social occasions for Polish American communities. Many of the customs associated with weddings were carried over or adapted from traditional Polish practices, but modifications were inevitable in the New World setting. In Poland, marriages were often arranged between families with the assistance of a proposer, or go-between. At first, some immigrant parents in Wisconsin continued to arrange marriages for their children, but the practice soon died out. The Polish custom of sending a matchmaker to propose marriage was not followed in Wisconsin. As the wedding day approached, however, the groomsmen went from farm to farm inviting the guests, much as in Poland.

In Portage County, wedding celebrations were typically long and lavish. The wedding ceremony usually took place in the morning. According to Portage County resident Michael Lisz, the musicians accompanied the wedding party to the church, following Polish custom. Afterward everyone returned to the bride's parents' farm for dancing and feasting. The dancing took place in the house if there was room, but more often in a barn or in a big tent set up on the lawn. In later years, wedding parties were held in dance halls, usually adjacent to a tavern. Once the first years of privation were past, Polish weddings proffered food and drink in abundance. Polonia farmer August Kluch recalled that when he was married, his father-in-law served the meat from a whole cow, chickens, beets, and head cheese; August, as the groom, provided sixteen barrels of beer, thirteen gallons of whiskey, wine, and soft drinks.

Dancing went on all day, with breaks for dinner and supper. Later in the evening, the "bride's dance" began. Men who wished to dance with the bride threw silver dollars onto heavy china plates. If the plate broke, the man got to dance with the bride, and afterward, the coins went to the young couple. After the bride's dance, the bride's veil was ceremoniously removed by the older women. This practice was derived from the Polish "capping" ceremony, in which the bride's headdress was replaced with the married woman's cap. The unveiling ritual in Wisconsin consisted of removing the veil and floral headpiece, then replacing the headpiece instead of putting on a cap. The women sang a traditional song about the joys and sorrows to come in the bride's new life, and accompanied it with copious weeping. The dancing and feasting continued long into the night and sometimes into the next day. The day after the wedding, or several days later, the bride and groom invited the wedding party, family, and close friends back for the *poprawiny*, or repetition. As in Poland, the *poprawiny* was a continuation of the wedding celebration, but for a more select group.

At the end of a long life, the dearest wish of many Polish immigrants was for a proper Christian burial. A major impetus behind the formation of Polish American fraternal organizations was to provide burial insurance so their members could be assured of just such a passage into eternity. After a death, the body was laid out in the house and people would sit up all night, talking and singing religious songs. In many Polish American communities, the funeral was held on the third or fourth day after death. The mourners met at the home on the morning of the funeral to bid farewell to the deceased before the coffin was closed. The funeral procession then formed outside the house and accompanied the coffin to church. After a Requiem Mass, the body was taken to the church cemetery and lowered into the grave. Afterward, mourners were invited to the home of the deceased for a festive meal.

LANGUAGE

Polish immigrants to Wisconsin usually arrived without any knowledge of English. In Polish communities, Polish was spoken everywhere and it remained the primary language in many areas until 1930 or later. In parts of Portage County, an immigrant could feel quite at home speaking nothing but Polish. Nevertheless, many Polish farmers spoke both Polish and English, and those from Prussian-occupied Poland usually spoke German as well. Their wives, however, who rarely ventured outside the Polish community, did not always learn to speak English. With each succeeding generation, the use of English grew and Polish diminished. Children of the earliest Polish immigrants often continued to prefer Polish to English, and their children usually spoke Polish until they went to school.

The Polish language spoken by immigrants and their children underwent changes as decades passed, resulting in the creation of a distinctive Polish American dialect. English words were incorporated into Polish, either because there was no Polish equivalent or for no obvious reason, probably just because they had become familiar. These English loan words were often given a Polish spelling and inflected according to Polish grammatical rules. For example, "farm," *gospodarswtwo* in Polish, was referred to as *farma* (plural, *farmy*), and a farmer was a *farmer*. Corn was *korna*. People did their shopping at a *sztor* (store), might have a suit made at the *szap krawiecki* (tailor shop), and stopped in at the local *salun* (saloon) for a drink with friends.

In many Polish communities, the turning point in the shift from Polish to English occurred around 1930, and it accelerated rapidly after World War II. Even in later years, remnants of Polish usage colored the English spoken in Polish communities. Some Polish expressions were translated literally into English. For example, a woman's maiden name was known as her name "from home." Other times, Polish grammatical constructions were carried over into English, and even people who didn't speak Polish sprinkled their speech with Polish words they had heard at home or in the neighborhood.

HEALTH AND HEALING

In nineteenth-century Poland, a peasant might never see a medical doctor. In the United States, physicians were more accessible and were usually called in cases of serious illness. Several Polish doctors advertised their services in Stevens Point's Polish newspaper, but many rural communities did not have their own doctor, and for serious illnesses a physician had to be brought from a neighboring town. For ordinary ailments, Polish women relied on a host of home remedies, including a number of herbal recipes brought from Poland. In Hofa Park, mothers would send their children out on summer days to pick blossoms that were used in winter for making tea, which served as a cough preventive. Goose lard, rabbit lard, honey, and horseradish also were valued for their medicinal properties. In Pulaski during the early twentieth century, milk was considered a general cure-all, and people dosed themselves with brandy to keep warm. Mrs. Julia Polczynski of Pulaski used whiskey and pepper to cure stomachache, a cold cloth dipped in vinegar and water tied around the head for headache, and a rub of goose grease mixed with turpentine for a chest cold. A tea brewed from dried linden flowers was used to treat asthma and bronchitis, while an infusion of chamomile flowers was thought to cure stomach cramps and colic in babies.

Second Sacred Heart Church in Polonia. The first church in the Portage County settlement of Polonia had been moved from Poland Corner (Ellis) in 1872 because of problems caused by nearby saloons. After it burned down in 1875, it was replaced by this stone structure.

WHi Image ID 34693

Third Sacred Heart Church in Polonia. Sacred Heart Parish grew rapidly and the old stone church proved inadequate. When this brick church was consecrated in 1903, it served some 2,400 parishioners. Seventy feet wide and 167 feet long, the new building was said to be the largest church in Wisconsin north of Milwaukee. It was struck by lightning in 1934 and was replaced by a fourth church, which still stands.

WHi Image ID 34692

Assumption of the Blessed Virgin Mary Church and Franciscan Monastery in Pulaski, ca. 1908. When the first Assumption Church became too small, parishioners began work on a much larger structure. After running out of funds, they built a roof over the basement and used this as a temporary church from 1908 until the new building was completed in 1931.

Pulaski Area Historical Society

This brick roadside shrine at the intersection of County Highways Z and I in the Portage County town of Sharon is typical of those that once dotted the landscape of Polish settlements in central and northeastern Wisconsin.

Portage County Historical Society

Parishioners gather at the corner of St. Augustine and Pulaski Streets in Pulaski, across from the church, ca. 1895.

Sura's Tavern in Independence, ca. 1911

Independence Public Library / Independence Area Historical Society

Threshing crews and equipment traveled from farm to farm. This picture was taken on the Paul Woychik farm near Independence.

Kwasniewski Photographs, UW-Milwaukee Libraries-Archives, 25598-2

Jan Stryszewski and his wife, photographed with their horses in front of a log barn in Armstrong Creek, 1926.

WHi Image ID 87493

The Martin Schulist family stands behind their clapboard-sided farmhouse in the town of Sharon, ca. 1905.

WHi Image ID 87495

The John Kuklinski family poses in front of their large frame farmhouse near Polonia, 1907.

WHi Image ID 87490

Family and neighbors gather to celebrate the wedding of Agnes Omernik and Joseph Lorbiecki at Polonia in 1916.

A funeral gathering for twelve-year old Hilary Marsolek in Independence, 1915. The deceased boy is pictured in the inset.

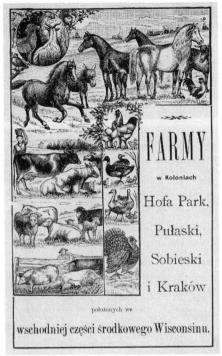

FARMY

w Koloniach

Hofa Park,

Pułaski,

Sobieski

i Kraków

położonych we

wschodniej części środkowego Wisconsinu.

WHi Image ID 41744

Cover of a pamphlet in Polish intended to encourage immigrants to settle in J. J. Hof's "colonies" of Hofa Park, Pulaski, Sobieski, and Krakow, northwest of Green Bay, ca. 1894.

WHi Image ID 87500

J. J. Hof Land Company branch office, Sobieski, 1894. Hof's main office was in Milwaukee, but he opened a branch office in Sobieski in the fall of 1894. He employed Polish agents to draw more Polish settlers to the area.

First grade class, St. Peter's School, Stevens Point. Nearly all Polish parishes had their own primary schools, which taught religion and Polish culture in addition to the "three Rs." Easy Polish words were written on the blackboard under the alphabet and the name of the school.

Facing page: First Communion was a major event in the lives of Polish American Catholic children. SS Peter and Paul parish in Independence was founded by Poles from Upper Silesia. This photo was taken ca. 1916–1917. The priest, Father Andrew Gara, had immigrated from Austrian Poland in 1885. He served as pastor of Holy Family parish in Poniatowski and Sacred Heart in Pine Creek, among others, before coming to SS Peter and Paul in 1901.

Portage County Historical Society

Independence Public Library / Independence Area Historical Society

MILWAUKEE: THREE SETTLEMENTS

Despite the large number of rural Polish settlements across Wisconsin, by far the greatest concentration of Poles was in Milwaukee County. Many Polish immigrants worked in Milwaukee before moving on to rural areas, and many more simply stayed. Even for farmers who had little experience of city life, the attractions were many: high-paying jobs, the promise of home ownership, Polish churches, and the proximity of fellow Poles.

According to some accounts, the first Pole in Milwaukee was a sixteen-year-old lad named Michael Skupniewicz, who arrived in 1846 and, after saving up five hundred dollars, moved to Dodge County, where he bought land near Beaver Dam. Historian Robert Caroon notes, however, that another Pole, Anthony Stupinski, had settled in Milwaukee with his family as early as 1842 or 1843. In any case, by 1847 several Polish families called Milwaukee home, and three years later there were at least sixteen Polish families in Milwaukee County.

Polish immigrants continued to trickle in during the 1850s, but their numbers did not become significant until after the Civil War. An 1874 article in the *Milwaukee Sentinel* estimated the city's Polish population at seven thousand. There was a rush of Polish immigration in the early 1880s, and by the end of the decade, Milwaukee's roughly thirty thousand Poles were second in number only to the fifty thousand Germans. The Polish population swelled to an estimated forty thousand in 1895 and reached seventy thousand in 1910. By this time, Poles had become a prominent and influential element of Milwaukee's citizenry. They dominated the southwestern section of the city and also occupied an East Side district between Brady Street and the Milwaukee River, as well as a fishing community on Jones Island. Seven of the city's twenty-nine Roman Catholic parishes were Polish. In addition, the Polish population boasted three free libraries, a hundred Polish societies and organizations, and five Polish newspapers.

More than 80 percent of Wisconsin's Polish immigrants came from the Prussian-governed areas of Poland, especially from East and West Prussia and the Grand Duchy of Poznań. According to the 1900 census, only 11 percent of Wisconsin's Poles were from the Russian partition and less than 9 percent from the Austrian partition. This set Wisconsin apart from other states with large Polish populations, where, on average, less than 40 percent of all Polish immigrants were from the German-speaking Prussian partition.

In 1866 some thirty families established Milwaukee's first Polish parish, which they named St. Stanislaus, after Poland's patron saint. The immigrant parishioners raised four thousand dollars and purchased a small Lutheran church on the corner of Fifth and Mineral Streets. Dedicated in March of 1866, St. Stanislaus was the second Polish parish in Wisconsin (after Sacred Heart in Polonia) and the first urban Polish parish in the United States. In September of 1868, the parish opened a grade school adjoining the church and engaged Sister M. Tyta, a member of the Order of School Sisters of Notre Dame, as its first teacher. This school followed, by four months, the dedication of a rudimentary Polish school in Panna Maria, Texas, making St. Stanislaus the second Polish parochial school in America.

Situated in the center of Milwaukee's rapidly expanding Polish neighborhood, St. Stanislaus was soon bursting at the seams. In 1871 a group of East Side Poles broke away and formed St. Hedwig's parish, but St. Stanislaus still needed room to grow. Under Father John Rodowicz, St. Stanislaus's parishioners commissioned a Chicago Polish architect to design a larger building. They paid him eight hundred dollars for plans, but when the new foundation began to crumble, the architect left town. The parish then hired a Milwaukee Polish architect, Leonard Schmidt-ner, who also went by the name Baron von Kowalski. In 1872 St. Stanislaus parish held an outdoor festival to celebrate the cornerstone laying. Booths were set up around the perimeter to sell refreshments and souvenirs. About a thousand dollars was raised to start a building fund for the new church. In addition, each parishioner was assessed thirty dollars. Father Rodowicz, parish president August Rudziński, and treasurer Józef Piszczek went from house to house collecting funds. Some parishioners gave fifty or a hundred dollars, and several gave their land as security for the twenty-thousand-dollar mortgage. In 1873 a large cream brick building with twin dome-topped towers was dedicated at Grove (now Fifth) and Mitchell Streets.

By this time, St. Stanislaus had about a thousand parishioners, representing four hundred families. As newly arrived Polish families moved into the neighborhood, it soon became apparent that the church could not accommodate them all. Less than ten years after St. Stanislaus's dedication, the new pastor, Father Jacek (Hyacinth) Gulski, concluded that the parish would have to be divided. At the congregation's annual meeting in 1882, it was determined that parishioners living west of Fifth Avenue (now Tenth Street) would form a new parish, to be called St. Hyacinth. Father Gulski oversaw the building of a new church on the corner of Becher Street and Tenth Avenue (now Fifteenth Street). Designed by prominent Milwaukee architect Henry Messmer, the cream brick structure was 136 feet long by 62 feet wide and seated eight hundred people. The dedication took place on April 1, 1883. The following year, Father Gulski moved to St. Hyacinth as pastor, leaving St. Stanislaus in the hands of Father Hipolit Górski. Father Górski oversaw further enlargement and improvement of St. Stanislaus. Each parishioner was assessed fifteen dollars, and by 1884 the parish was free of debt, with $3,662.66 in the treasury. After building a new school in 1889, however, St. Stanislaus once again owed money, to the tune of twenty-eight thousand dollars. In addition to contributing for their own expenses, St. Stanislaus parishioners were assessed ten dollars, this time to help build yet another new church for Milwaukee's burgeoning Polish population.

St. Josaphat's, which later became the largest Polish parish in Wisconsin, began as an offshoot of St. Stanislaus in 1888. The original church burned down the following year, and a second building was erected, at a cost of thirty thousand dollars. Not ten years later, the congregation was outgrowing its new home. St. Josaphat's visionary rector, Father Wilhelm Grutza, undertook the building of an even larger church to accommodate his expanding flock. Father Grutza, who had visited Rome, conceived an ambitious plan to replicate St. Peter's Basilica in Milwaukee. He engaged Erhard Brielmaier, a local German architect, to design a scaled-down version of St. Peter's. The plans were nearly complete when Father Grutza learned that the U.S. Custom House and Post Office in Chicago was to be demolished and the building materials sold. Father Grutza purchased the entire structure for less than twenty-two thousand dollars and asked Brielmaier to create a new design incorporating the Custom House building materials. Father Grutza had the materials shipped to Milwaukee on five hundred railroad flat cars. Parishioners contributed generously, and some mortgaged their own homes to raise funds. The parish broke ground in 1896. Father Grutza, a trained blacksmith, served as construction foreman, and parishioners supplied most of the labor.

The church was finally dedicated in 1901. At the time, the parish had more than twelve thousand members, and four thousand people attended the dedication. Unfortunately, the strain of building and raising funds had taken its toll on Father Grutza's health. He was present for the dedication ceremonies but too ill to participate. He died a month later, leaving the parish with a magnificent house of worship and a five-hundred-thousand-dollar debt. By 1909 the church was faced with foreclosure. In 1910 the Milwaukee Archdiocese turned St. Josaphat over to the Conventual Franciscan Fathers of Buffalo, New York. The Franciscans assumed four hundred thousand dollars of the debt and split the remainder among other Milwaukee-area congregations. In 1925 the parishioners finally retired the debt. Due to the longstanding financial difficulties, however, the church's huge interior was still unfinished. In 1926, the pastor, Father Felix Baran, contracted with Italian artist Gonippo Raggi to complete the interior decoration, which included murals depicting scenes from Christian and Polish history. In 1929 Pope Pius XI declared St. Josaphat a minor basilica — a distinction reserved for large and finely decorated churches that are also important centers of faith. St. Josaphat's was only the third church in the United States, and the first Polish church, to receive the designation of basilica. In 1973, it was listed on the National Register of Historic Places.

KĘPA KASZUBÓW: THE EAST SIDE

Milwaukee's Polish settlement, estimated at about fifty families in 1866, continued to grow. Drawn northward by the availability of undeveloped land and industrial jobs along the Milwaukee River, Polish immigrants began to settle the swampy land between the Milwaukee River and today's East Brady Street in the late 1860s. Most of this neighborhood's early settlers came from the Kaszuby region of northern Poland, along the Baltic seacoast. Many were from the area around Puck, and some came from the Hel peninsula, a long spit of land extending into the Baltic Sea. The Kaszubes spoke a distinctive dialect of Polish. Unlike most other Poles, and even unlike Kaszubes from farther inland, the coastal Kaszubes made their living by fishing. Their settlement on Milwaukee's East Side was often referred to as Kępa Kaszubów (Islet of the Kaszubes). Not having their own church in the early years, they attended services at St. Stanislaus. In 1870, at the same time as the parishioners of St. Stanislaus decided to build a larger church on the corner of Fifth and

Mitchell Streets, about forty Polish families living on the East Side resolved to establish a new church in their own territory.

In the spring of 1871, with the help of August Rudziński, the South Side community leader who had helped to fund St. Stanislaus Church, a group of East Side Polish settlers acquired three muddy lots on the banks of a deep ravine at Brady Street between Franklin Place and Humboldt Avenue. Work began immediately on the construction of a new brick-faced church. The building was dedicated on October 17, 1871, the feast day of the parish's patron saint, St. Hedwig. The *Milwaukee Sentinel* estimated that there were about seventy Polish families living in the neighborhood at the time. Following the building of St. Hedwig's Church, the surrounding area developed rapidly. Two nearby streets were named after Polish heroes — Pulaski Street and Sobieski Street. By 1888 the area around St. Hedwig's was solidly built up, and by 1910 it was almost completely developed. The residents were virtually all Polish.

The dense, self-contained neighborhood that grew up around St. Hedwig's was a veritable urban village, characterized by small, closely spaced houses and numerous outbuildings. In 1880 the *Sentinel* noted that the inhabitants of the gully that later became Pulaski Street leased the land on which their houses stood. When the leases were up, the houses were moved and new ones were put up in their place. According to the *Sentinel*, refuse was thrown into the gully from the neighboring houses, and orders to clean it up went unheeded. Eventually the gully was filled in and paved over, but its colorful history accounts for Pulaski Street's still-crooked contours.

As the East Side settlement began to spread across the Milwaukee River, St. Hedwig's parish split in two. In 1893 a new Polish church, St. Casimir's, was founded about one and a half miles to the north, on the northeast corner of North Bremen and East Clarke Streets. All the St. Hedwig's families living west of the Milwaukee River were requested to join the new parish. St. Casimir's grew rapidly, and within two years it surpassed St. Hedwig's in membership. The Polish settlement around St. Casimir's, west of the Milwaukee River, continued to spread north-ward, and yet another parish was formed. St. Mary of Czestochowa parish was incorporated in 1907 and dedicated a new church building in May of 1908.

THE POLISH SOUTH SIDE

Meanwhile, Milwaukee's original Polish settlement expanded from its nucleus around St. Stanislaus Church, and it was here, on the South Side, that the city's largest and most populous Polish neighborhood developed. Located within walking distance of industrial plants in the Menomonee Valley, the area offered easy access to jobs and an abundance of inexpensive house lots. Newly erected church steeples towered over the blocks of workers' cottages that advanced steadily to the south and west.

In 1888, only five years after St. Hyacinth parish split off from St. Stanislaus, St. Hyacinth gave rise to its own daughter parish, St. Vincent de Paul, at Mitchell and Sixteenth Avenue (now South Twenty-first Street). Each of St. Hyacinth's families was assessed five dollars or more to fund St. Vincent's combined church and school building. By century's end, the congregation again needed more space and engaged the South Side's leading Polish architect, Bernard Kolpacki, who designed an imposing 182-foot tan brick church reminiscent of the German Renaissance style. The contractor was another Pole, parish member Sylvester Wabiszewski.

By 1892 Milwaukee was home to an estimated thirty-five thousand Poles. Five Polish parishes embraced at least five thousand families, and some four thousand children attended Polish parish schools. In 1893 St. Hyacinth and St. Josaphat congregations spawned yet another parish, SS Cyril and Methodius, situated on a picturesque triangular parcel at the intersection of West Hayes Avenue, West Windlake Avenue, and Tenth Avenue (now South Fifteenth Street). Bernard Kolpacki, a parish member, designed an imposing cream brick Victorian Gothic church, and Father Jan F. Szukalski moved from St. Michael's Church in Beaver Dam to serve as the parish's first priest.

As Milwaukee's immigrant population swelled, still more Polish parishes sprang up to accommodate the faithful. In 1907 Father Louis Jurasinski, assistant pastor to Father Szukalski at SS Cyril and Methodius, organized a new parish, which he named St. John Kanty. A school, attached to the church building, was opened soon after, with the School Sisters of Notre Dame in charge. St. John Kanty later gave rise to two more Polish parishes, St. Alexander's and St. Helen's. St. Alexander's combined church and school building, designed by Polish architects Leon and Francis Gurda, was erected on Holt Avenue between South Fifteenth

Place and South Sixteenth Street in 1925. St. Helen's parish, organized in 1925, dedicated a combined church and school in 1927.

Meanwhile, St. Hyacinth's spun off yet another important Polish parish, St. Adalbert. In 1908, the newly organized congregation purchased five lots at the corner of Becher and South Nineteenth Streets. On February 28, 1909, the parish dedicated a combination church and eight-room school, and completed a rectory soon afterward. The School Sisters of Notre Dame presided over St. Adalbert's school for the first year, but in August of 1910 the parish's new pastor, the Reverend Wacław (Wenceslaus) Kruszka, brought a Polish order, the Sisters of St. Joseph, from Stevens Point to take over the teaching. The school reached its peak enrollment in 1924, when twenty-three sisters taught 1,585 children.

From 1909 until 1937, Father Kruszka made St. Adalbert's a focus of controversy within the Archdiocese by his independent stance toward the Roman Catholic Church hierarchy. Father Kruszka was the younger half-brother of Michael Kruszka, editor of the *Kuryer Polski* newspaper and a controversial figure in his own right. Born in Słabomierz, in the Prussian partition, Wacław was educated in a German grammar school and a Polish high school. In 1883 he entered the Jesuit Order at Stara Wieś in the Austrian partition. Ten years later, as a result of disputes and misunderstandings, Kruszka was dismissed from the Jesuits. Since this rendered him vulnerable to conscription in the Prussian army, he decided to follow his older brother, Michael, to Milwaukee. He entered St. Francis Seminary and was ordained by Archbishop Katzer in 1895. After an initial assignment in St. Josaphat parish, Kruszka was sent to Ripon, Wisconsin, where he founded a small Polish parish named St. Wenceslaus.

In quiet Ripon, the energetic Kruszka began writing on a variety of religious and cultural topics, publishing some of his writings in his brother's newspaper. Noticing how soon the contributions of Polish pioneer settlers had been forgotten, Kruszka also started conducting research for a history of Polish immigrants in the United States. In 1901 he began serializing his history in the *Kuryer*. After receiving corrections and additional contributions from readers, Kruszka published the entire history in thirteen volumes between 1905 and 1908. Although later scholars have criticized Kruszka's work for inaccuracies and bias, Kruszka's history broke new ground at the time and still preserves important source material that otherwise would have been lost.

An ardent nationalist, Wacław Kruszka was troubled by apparent anti-Polish bias in the American church hierarchy and became an out-spoken advocate for the appointment of Polish bishops. A national Polish Catholic convention in 1901 selected him to represent their grievances to the pope. He went to Rome in 1903 and returned in 1904 with a promise of help from Pope Pius X. Despite the pope's assurances, however, Kruszka found the American bishops, who were mainly of Irish and German descent, as unresponsive as ever. When Kruszka's efforts failed to meet with any action from the pope, extreme dissidents held the first synod of the Polish National Catholic Church and elected their own bishop, Francis Hodur of Scranton, Pennsylvania. In spite of Kruszka's opposition to the Roman Catholic Church hierarchy, however, he never wavered in his allegiance to the Roman Catholic faith.

At the same time that he was battling for greater recognition for Polish priests in the church hierarchy, Kruszka was waging a personal campaign for a transfer from the obscure Ripon parish to a more promi-nent post. His efforts were finally rewarded in 1909, when he was ap-pointed pastor of St. Adalbert parish in Milwaukee. The campaign for a Polish bishop, in which Kruszka played a leading role, finally resulted in the appointment of Edward Kozłowski as auxiliary bishop of Milwau-kee in 1913. Although it wasn't a full bishophood, Kozłowski's appoint-ment was greeted with jubilation by Milwaukee's Polish Catholics. An estimated fifty thousand people lined Mitchell Street to catch a glimpse of their new leader on the cold January day of his consecration. Unfor-tunately, Kozłowski died two years later. Sadness over his loss was some-what alleviated, however, by the appointment, in the same year, of Chicago's Polish auxiliary, Peter Paul Rhode, as bishop to the Green Bay diocese.

Meanwhile, at St. Adalbert's, Father Kruszka's colorful preaching style and dedication to the needy earned him the affection of his parish-ioners. A familiar figure on Milwaukee's South Side, he delivered stirring addresses on patriotic themes at many Polish community celebrations. A patriot as well as a priest, Kruszka served as chairman of the local recruiting committee for the Polish Army during the First World War. Kruszka oversaw the construction of a new and larger Romanesque church in 1931. He continued to serve St. Adalbert's parish until his death in 1937.

As Milwaukee's Polish settlement expanded to the south and west, St. Adalbert's gave rise to its own daughter parishes — St. Barbara, at

2075 South Thirty-second Street (1921–1924), and St. Mary Magdalen, at South Nineteenth Street just north of Harrison (1925). Both St. Barbara and St. Mary Magdalen were constructed as combined church and school buildings. The organization of the parishes of St. Ignatius in 1926 and Blessed Sacrament in 1927 brought the total number of Polish Roman Catholic parishes in Milwaukee to seventeen and marked the end of the era of new Polish parishes.

Milwaukee's residential growth was accompanied by commercial development. Mitchell Street was known as "the Polish Grand Avenue" — a reference to Milwaukee's major downtown thoroughfare. Grocery stores, butcher shops, and bakeries bustled with Polish-speaking customers. Saloons took the place of the old Polish village inn as places to relax, socialize, and keep up with local news. Drugstores, dry-good stores, hardware stores, livery stables, notary publics, and real estate offices were just some of the other businesses that catered to the needs of neighborhood residents. As the line of settlement advanced southward, another busy commercial district grew up along Lincoln Avenue in the shadow of St. Josaphat's Basilica.

JONES ISLAND

Milwaukee's third Polish neighborhood was a marshy peninsula known as Jones Island. Situated near the entrance to Milwaukee's harbor, it was settled by Kaszubian fishermen from the Hel peninsula on Poland's Baltic coast. According to local legend, the first Kaszube to set foot on Jones Island was a fisherman named Valentine Struck, who visited before the Civil War and then went home. Struck returned to Jones Island with his family in the late 1860s; his son, Felix, was the first baby born on the island, in 1870. It wasn't long before other Kaszubes followed the Strucks to Jones Island. In 1872 Jacob Muza and his wife arrived, along with a group that included John Stein and his wife, Michael Budzisz, and Andreas Kohnke. Muza, the group's leader, bought a house from Gottlieb Truher, a German who had settled on the island two years earlier. Although Truher gave Muza a bill of sale for the house, he had no title to the land under it, setting a precedent that produced unfortunate consequences for subsequent generations of Jones Islanders. Muza and the others set to work filling in the swampy land and building a wooden breakwater to hold back the lake. When he wasn't fishing, Jacob Muza worked in a steel-rolling mill, and he also opened a grocery store and saloon. Muza and his neighbors worked tirelessly to fill in the low-lying land, while Muza helped new arrivals find plots to settle on, all without benefit of legal title.

Kaszubian settlers were joined by Germans from the area near Szczecin (in German, *Stettin*), about two hundred miles west of Hel. Jones Island's German inhabitants belonged to St. Stephen's Lutheran Church, while the Kaszubes worshiped at St. Stanislaus, but the two groups lived and worked side by side for as long as the island way of life lasted. In the early years, Jones Island fishermen fished in shallow water with "pond" or "pound" nets, which were stretched between poles driven into the lake bottom and could be set and lifted from rowboats. As the fishing industry developed, some fishermen were able to afford sailboats, which allowed them to venture into deeper water with larger gill nets. Later, the fishermen began to use steam-powered fishing tugs, first made of wood, then steel. Initially the nets had to be hauled aboard by hand; in time, engine-driven lifts made the job easier. Most of the fish were sold locally to customers and dealers who waited on the docks for the boats to come in. In later years, however, surplus fish was packed in ice and shipped to Chicago.

By 1880 there were some twenty houses on Jones Island and by 1900, perhaps two hundred. All told, about fifteen hundred people lived in weather-beaten houses in the urban fishing village that had grown up without any discernible plan on the mile-long peninsula. By 1896 Jones Island had become the center of Milwaukee's fishing industry. Between 1909 and 1916 nearly two million pounds of fish were caught each year, and in 1917, about 175 islanders made their livelihoods by fishing while roughly the same number were engaged in selling fish. Some of the fish were sold fresh from island shops or delivered by horse and wagon to stores and saloons on the mainland. Many fish peddlers also owned smokehouses, and there was a lively business in smoked fish. Jones Island was a popular destination for mainland residents, who came both to buy fish and to carouse in the dozen or so taverns that flourished away from the city center. Along with catching and selling fish, net making and repair were essential components of the Jones Island fishing industry. During the winter, when fishing was impossible, island men worked on their nets and supplemented their incomes by laboring in mainland industries.

For more than twenty years, Kaszubian and German fishermen

made their homes, unmolested, on reclaimed land that seemingly belonged to nobody in particular, but the situation was not to last. The Illinois Steel Company held title to much of the island, and beginning in 1896 the company stepped up efforts to evict the "squatters" who had made it habitable. Through a lengthy series of much-publicized legal proceedings and forcible evictions, one by one, the island residents were driven out of their houses. Meanwhile, in 1915–1916, the City of Milwaukee began proceedings to purchase the northern half of Jones Island for harbor improvements and sewage storage. At the same time, overfishing and low prices for fish made commercial fishing increasingly less profitable. In 1920 only twenty families remained on Jones Island, and two years later, there were eight. Captain Felix Struck, the first Kaszube born on Jones Island, was the last to leave it when he was forced to close his popular Harbor saloon in 1944.

OUTSIDE MILWAUKEE: THE INDUSTRIAL SOUTHEAST

The growth of meat-processing and manufacturing industries in Cudahy, South Milwaukee, Kenosha, and Racine attracted large numbers of Poles to Wisconsin's southeastern counties in the 1890s. Poles from Milwaukee began to buy up inexpensive lots in South Milwaukee between 1891 and 1894. After attending a German church, the Poles formed St. Adalbert parish in 1898 and soon opened a school under the supervision of a lay teacher who was also the organist. Polish families living in nearby Cudahy traveled to South Milwaukee to attend St. Adalbert's until founding their own parish, Holy Family, in 1900.

In 1901, Poles and Lithuanians living in Kenosha incorporated St. Casimir parish, dedicating a brick church designed by Polish architect H. A. Kulas of Milwaukee two years later. The first pastor was a Lithuanian, Father Ambrozajtys; he was succeeded by a Pole, Father Wiktor Zaręczny, who very soon began to organize a Polish parish in Racine.

Poles had begun settling in Racine about 1890. In 1904 a group of Poles incorporated the parish of St. Stanislaus Bishop and Martyr. On February 24, 1908, Archbishop Messmer dedicated a new church building. The parish opened a school in 1915, with the Sisters of St. Joseph from Stevens Point engaged to teach. More than 80 percent of the Poles in Racine County lived in the city of Racine, where they congregated on the far south side. Other Poles lived in Caledonia or the Lakeside section of Mount Pleasant, where, along with Italians, Hungarians, Slovaks, Rus-

sians, and Lithuanians, they worked for the Case South Works or Lakeside Malleable Iron. Racine supported a number of Polish organizations,
including a chapter of the Polish National Alliance, organized in 1905,
and a nest of the Polish Falcons. Most of the groups met in the Polish
Hall at Mead and DeKoven Streets.

CREATING THE URBAN VILLAGE

Milwaukee's Polish neighborhoods, on both the South and the East Side,
shared distinctive characteristics, partly derived from their Old World
heritage. Most Polish peasants were accustomed to living in close-knit
villages, where houses clustered tightly together around an open space or
along a single street. Behind each wooden cottage was a yard with a barn
and other outbuildings. The yard served as a work area and as home to
the family poultry. In the garden next to, in front of, or behind the house,
the family cultivated a combination of vegetables, herbs, and flowers.

When they moved to American cities, the majority of Polish immigrants eschewed tenement buildings in favor of small, detached houses.
Contemporary social reformers complained that the yards of Polish immigrants exhibited conditions more befitting a village farmyard than a
city lot — muddy, strewn with refuse, and often sporting barns or chicken
coops. Vegetable gardens were squeezed between the front and rear
houses. Chickens, ducks, and geese were common; some householders
even kept pigs and cows.

Polish immigrants brought with them an intense desire to own property. Owing their livelihoods to the soil, Polish peasants valued land ownership above almost everything, except perhaps their Catholic faith. In
Milwaukee, Poles rapidly achieved an extraordinarily high rate of home
ownership, especially considering their modest incomes. Typically, a
family began by building a small cottage on a narrow house lot, and then,
as soon as finances permitted, they expanded it by the least expensive
means. A 1911 study by the British Board of Trade described a typical
building sequence and the crowding that resulted:

In the South Side district, where a large class of the poorer section of the Poles live, the custom is to erect first a four-roomed

frame dwelling. When this has been paid for, it is raised on posts
to allow a semi-basement dwelling to be constructed under-
neath, the lower portion being banked round with clay to afford
protection against the snow in winter. This basement or the
upstairs flat is then let by the owner, who, as soon as his funds
permit, substitutes brick walls for the timber of the basement,
but the ambition of a Polish house-owner is not crowned until
he is able to have cement walks and iron railings in front of his
house. In the above district a very large number of these semi-
basements of wood can be seen, and although the outer aspect
of the dwellings is not unpleasing, they are in general undeni-
ably insanitary, being damp, as the floor of the basement rests
on the ground. Such houses, which when completed, contain
eight rooms, are frequently occupied by four or five families as
well as boarders, and as Polish families are generally large this
overcrowding is a serious evil.

The distinctive type of dwelling that resulted from jacking the house
up and building a high basement beneath it came to be known as a
"Polish flat," since it was common in Polish neighborhoods. Other
homeowners expanded their houses by adding onto the back or raising
the roof, although these methods could be more costly. In addition to
raising cottages or adding on to buildings, many Polish immigrants
increased the residential capacity of their properties by constructing
second, and even third, dwellings at the rear of their narrow lots. These
rear cottages were usually one-story frame structures built on wooden
pile foundations. In many cases, an old cottage was moved from the front
of the property to the rear when a new house was built. Alternatively,
a small cottage might be built at the rear of a lot in the expectation of
building a larger house in front later on. Other times, front and rear
cottages were built or moved to the lot at the same time. For newly
arrived Polish immigrants, pride in owning their own homes outweighed
any concern for privacy. In fact, the strong sense of community that
came from living in close contact with neighbors was generally viewed
as a good thing by the Poles.

An 1874 *Milwaukee Sentinel* article about Milwaukee's Polish citizens
offered these observations on the East Side (First Ward) and South Side
neighborhoods:

There is little observable difference, except that of size, between the settlements of the First Ward and South Side. In both, the houses are generally small; very frequently one of these little cabins has three or four families crowded into it. Usually the first money they can call their own is put into the purchase of a lot, or part of a lot, on which they mean to erect a house as soon as possible. They have a strong prejudice against paying rent.

Indeed, while Poles showed no hesitation in borrowing money to finance a house purchase, they typically felt driven to liquidate the debt as quickly as possible. Sharing space with extended family members and renting out accommodations to strangers allowed them to pay off their loans quickly or to generate income for improvements. Polish building and loan societies, known as *skarby*, offered short-term mortgages, generally for six years, but these were sometimes paid off even sooner.

Milwaukee's Polish neighborhoods were meant for walking. Residential and commercial buildings stood side by side. Retail stores in Polish neighborhoods were usually small, family-owned establishments. Grocery stores sold canned goods, bakery items, and dairy products, while meat markets, or butcher shops, sold meat and cold cuts. Regular customers bought their groceries "on the book," that is, on account. In most cases, the owners lived in an apartment over the store, which was simply called by the proprietor's surname, such as "Janowski's," "Michalak's," or "Tutkowski's."

The informal center of social life in immigrant communities was the neighborhood tavern or saloon. The saloon was the "poor man's club," where residents gathered to exchange news, engage in gossip and discussion, and find respite from the daily round of hard work. The owner often lived with his family in an apartment over the tavern. As entrepreneurs, saloon proprietors enjoyed a special status in the community. Since tavern owners handled substantial amounts of cash, they were in a position to lend money and hold mortgages. They frequently ascended to positions as officers in the mutual aid societies and sometimes entered into politics.

A logical outgrowth of Milwaukee's ethnic parishes and fraternal organizations was the formation of social service institutions, most of which were connected with the Catholic church. In the late nineteenth and early twentieth centuries, it was not uncommon for a child to lose one or both parents, and a single parent was often hard-pressed to take care of young children while earning a living. Financial hardship could render even married couples unable to care for their children. Children who had no relatives to take them in were consigned to an orphan asylum, usually run by a church organization. The prevailing view was that children should be reared in their parents' faith, and among Polish immigrants, there was a strong feeling that Polish children should be cared for in Polish orphanages.

Before 1907, the Felician Sisters had founded homes for orphans in Polonia and Manitowoc, Wisconsin. For some time, Milwaukee children were sent to one of these institutions, but as they became overcrowded, Monsignor Hyacinth Gulski, pastor of St. Hyacinth parish, sought to establish a Polish orphanage in Milwaukee. He aroused the interest of the Felicians, who raised funds to buy a ten-acre tract of land bounded by South Eighteenth and Twentieth Streets, West Euclid, and Ohio. They hired architect H. Esser and appealed to the community for construction costs, estimated at one hundred thousand dollars. Frank Niezorawski, a Polish contractor, was engaged to construct the building. The St. Joseph Orphan Asylum was dedicated on June 14, 1908. The orphanage became a substitute family for thousands of Polish children between the ages of three and sixteen. The Sisters saw to it that the children in their care received religious education as well as training in domestic and vocational skills. St. Joseph's maintained its own grade school and sent selected graduates on to one of several parochial high schools. After World War II, the Felician Sisters, together with Father A. A. Kosubucki of St. Alexander's parish, took the lead in building St. Francis Hospital next door to the orphanage. A group of more than 250 Polish women formed an auxiliary to raise funds, and prominent members of the Polish community made up the board. Milwaukee's Francis Gurda, an American-born Pole, was appointed architect.

Milwaukee's Polish Catholics derived comfort from living in close-knit neighborhoods, and they sought assurance that they would remain together in eternity as well. At first, parishioners of St. Stanislaus shared Holy Trinity Cemetery with several other Catholic congregations, but as early as 1888, they persuaded Archbishop M. Heiss of Milwaukee to buy thirty acres of land just south of Holy Trinity Cemetery so that the Poles could have their own burial ground. Consecrated as St. Adalbert's, it was also known as the Polish Union Cemetery, since it served all the Polish parishes. The original grounds soon proved too small, and the cemetery was enlarged several times by additional purchases. By 1946 it occupied more than one hundred acres and contained an estimated forty-six thousand burials, which included many of Milwaukee's most prominent Polish lawyers, doctors, and businessmen. Polish priests were buried in a special section of the cemetery, with a chapel adjoining. After the First World War, a separate section was set aside for war veterans; during World War II, this was expanded and another soldiers' section was opened in a new area of the cemetery.

As Polish immigrants settled in to American life, they and their children were anxious to be recognized as loyal Americans as well as patriotic Poles. Revolutionary War heroes Kazimierz Pułaski and Tadeusz Kościuszko embodied Poland's contribution to American freedom especially well. Their names were given to organizations, towns, streets, parks, bridges, highways, and schools around the country. One way for Polish communities to declare their ethnic pride was to erect public monuments commemorating their national heroes. Wisconsin was in the forefront of this movement.

In July 1890, the city of Milwaukee bought twenty-six acres of swampy woods for one hundred thousand dollars and spent an additional fifty thousand dollars to make it into a park. It was first called Coleman Park, then Lincoln Avenue Park. After intensive lobbying by the city's Poles, the city renamed it Kosciuszko Park in 1900. Two years later, the park was enlarged by the purchase of an additional 10.8 acres. For families short of living space, Kosciuszko Park was the neighborhood backyard. As the South Side's great outdoor public space, it became a popular destination for outings and picnics, as well as the site of numerous national holiday celebrations, outdoor concerts, and other public events.

In 1901 a special committee was formed to raise funds for a monument to Tadeusz Kościuszko in Kosciuszko Park. The committee included representatives of the major Polish organizations, including the powerful Polish National Alliance. Most of the money was raised from individual donations, many of twenty-five cents, and some as little as five cents. Gaetano Trentanove, a well-known Florentine sculptor who had once lived in Milwaukee, was selected to create the memorial. At his workshop in Florence, Trentanove cast a fifteen-foot-high equestrian statue of the Polish hero and shipped it, in two parts, to Milwaukee. The statue was set on a granite base at the north end of Kosciuszko Park, near

Becher Street. An estimated sixty thousand people attended the unveiling on June 18, 1905. Polish-born Archbishop Albin Symon, visiting the United States on a papal mission, delivered the principal oration. Milwaukee's Mayor Rose and Father Hyacinth Gulski also addressed the crowd. In 1951 the monument was moved to a more central location facing Lincoln Avenue; the rededication was a festive event, with some twenty-five thousand people present.

In Stevens Point, a monument to Brigadier General Kazimierz Pułaski, "father of the American cavalry," was dedicated on October 11, 1929 — the 150th anniversary of Pułaski's death. Governor Walter J. Kohler spoke at the ceremony in McGlachlin Park, where the bronze bust stands on a marble foundation. Another Pułaski memorial was unveiled in Milwaukee's Pulaski Park on October 17, 1931. As with the Kosciuszko monument twenty-six years earlier, a special committee raised the funds, and many Polish organizations contributed to the twenty-three-foot-high statue mounted on a granite shaft. The dedication ceremony, attended by an estimated thirty thousand people, was preceded by a two-mile-long parade. Speakers included Governor Philip La Follette, Mayor Daniel W. Hoan, and the Polish consul general from Chicago. The following year, a bronze bust of Pułaski was dedicated in neighboring Cudahy's Pulaski Park.

ORGANIZING COMMUNITY LIFE

Facing economic hardship in the best of times, Polish immigrants were especially vulnerable in the face of financial setbacks. Without the support of the Polish village community, the disability or death of a breadwinner could spell catastrophe for a family on the edge. Rather than be forced to accept institutional charity, Polish immigrants formed a variety of mutual benefit societies that provided at least a modest death benefit for their members. Although their primary purpose was insurance, these fraternal benefit societies also brought people together for social events, including meetings, picnics, and dances. Most of the fraternal groups were national organizations with regional governance structures and local lodges that also served as social clubs and provided educational resources. They offered an ethnic alternative to American societies like the Freemasons, and they were similar to fraternal organizations that were prevalent among many other ethnic groups, including Germans, Scandinavians, and Italians. Ambitious Polish immigrants could aspire to positions of influence within the organizations, and competition for status was sometimes intense.

The earliest national Polish fraternal organization was the Polish Roman Catholic Union of America (PRCUA), founded in 1873 in Detroit. The largest was the Polish National Alliance (PNA). After an organizational meeting in Detroit, the PRCUA held its second convention the following year in Chicago, and its third convention in 1875 in Milwaukee. The Polish National Alliance, organized in Philadelphia in 1880, moved its headquarters to Chicago within a few years. The Polish Falcons of America, a fraternal organization dedicated to physical fitness, was organized in Chicago in 1887.

All of these organizations had chapters in Milwaukee and in other Wisconsin communities. Milwaukee's first local PNA society, Group No. 14, was founded not long after the inception of the PNA and consisted of members of the Kosciuszko Guard. A second society, Group No. 54, composed of members of the Moniuszko Choir, soon followed, and more groups sprang up in rapid succession. In 1905 seven groups comprised Council No. 8, based on the South Side; by 1946 Council 8 embraced twenty-five groups from Milwaukee's South Side, West Allis, Cudahy, and South Milwaukee, plus an additional seven groups from other parts of Wisconsin. In 1942 Council 8 acquired its own headquarters — the former Polonia Hall at 809 West Burnham Street. A second Milwaukee PNA council, Council No. 115, was organized in 1915; it included five groups from Milwaukee's north side, as well as two La Crosse societies. The first PRCU group in Milwaukee was founded in 1907, but more soon followed, and by 1946 Milwaukee had more than thirty local societies.

Milwaukee was also the birthplace and headquarters of two national Polish fraternal organizations. The Association of Poles in America originated in the summer of 1895 when several Milwaukee chapters of the Polish Roman Catholic Union decided to start a separate organization. Within ten years, the association had grown to embrace seventy-five societies, half of which were in Wisconsin. By 1920 there were 178 groups in Wisconsin, Illinois, Michigan, Ohio, Pennsylvania, Indiana, New York, and New Jersey. The Association of Poles was the largest Polish fraternal organization in Wisconsin.

Michael Kruszka and the *Kuryer Polski* were involved in the 1911 founding of another national fraternal benefit society, the Federation of Polish Catholic Laymen in America, which aimed to obtain representation for Poles in the church hierarchy and to create Polish dioceses headed by bishops of Polish extraction. Like other fraternal organizations, it also provided death benefits to members. In 1913, the Milwaukee-based organization changed its name to the Federation of Poles in America, and, in 1924, to Federation Life Insurance of America. It continued for more than eighty years, before merging with the Polish Roman Catholic Union of America in 2005.

Numerous societies, clubs, veterans' posts, and other organizations were formed either for specific purposes or to participate in the general activity of the Polish community. These included the Polish Falcons and, at various times, special-interest groups such as mounted "knight" societies, the Polish Old Settlers Club, the Polish-American Citizens' Club, the Małopolan Club for persons hailing from the region of Little Poland, the Polish Book Club, and a variety of singing and dramatic circles.

Together with the church, the Polish fraternal orders, lodges, societies, and clubs provided a framework for community life. By 1910 there were some eighty different Polish organizations in Milwaukee. Many people belonged to more than one, but for the most part, the groups operated independently of one another. In 1928, a special committee was organized to commemorate the tenth anniversary of Poland's independence. Instead of disbanding the committee after its work was completed, it was decided to make it the basis of a permanent umbrella organization. Representatives of 106 Polish organizations convened on April 28, 1929, at the South Side Armory hall and adopted a plan for creating the Casimir Pulaski Council of Milwaukee. The group's wide-ranging activities embraced education, social welfare, and the arts. It lobbied to introduce Polish courses in high schools, at the Milwaukee Vocational School, and at the University of Wisconsin in Milwaukee and Madison. It was also instrumental in having the name Pulaski given to one of the city's largest and most modern public high schools. For many years, the Pulaski Council conducted a summer school at Kosciuszko Park with enrollments that sometimes reached five hundred. The Pulaski Council also provided aid to needy families and worked to alleviate the problem of juvenile delinquency in the Polish community. The council's civic improvements committee strove to improve transportation, safety, park facilities, and other matters affecting the city's Polish inhabitants, particularly on the South Side. The council was also active in various patriotic relief efforts during the Second World War.

In contrast to some other ethnic groups, Polish immigrant women took an active part in community life. From the earliest years, they participated in a variety of church groups and campaigned for social causes. Some of the male-dominated Polish fraternal organizations allowed women to participate on a limited basis, but reserved full membership for men. Women responded by forming associations of their own. One of the oldest, and the largest, was the Polish Women's Alliance, founded in Chicago in 1898. At a time when American women could not vote, the Polish Women's Alliance stood for the right of women to pursue higher education, enter the professions, and purchase life insurance under their own names. In 1910, when the organization held its eighth convention in Milwaukee, the PWA had 103 local groups in seven states. At that same convention, the PWA established its own weekly newspaper, *Głos Polek* (The Polish Women's Voice), which is still in existence as a quarterly magazine. The Polish Women's Alliance established its first Milwaukee group in 1905. By 1912, there were 600 members in Milwaukee. Besides providing life insurance, the PWA was active in social and civic affairs. They held lectures and classes, and also worked with the city's Sanitation League to improve conditions in Polish neighborhoods. On May 5, 1912, the *Milwaukee Journal* wrote, "Besides their complete organization they have the tact, the ability and the will to do what they see is best for their people and their part of the city."

IN DEFENSE OF FREEDOM

In 1874 Milwaukee Poles organized the first Polish military unit in the United States: the Kosciuszko Guard, or Company K. The organizer and first captain was August Rudziński. About one hundred men from St. Stanislaus parish responded to the initial call for volunteers, and they drilled on Sunday afternoons in the parish hall at St. Stanislaus. Since it was the second militia company in the city of Milwaukee, it was given the letter *B*. In 1877 Francis J. Borchardt was selected as captain. Eight years later, in 1885, the Kosciuszko Guard purchased two lots on South Sixth

Street and began to raise funds for an armory building. The South Side
Armory, popularly known as Kosciuszko Hall, was designed by Bernard
Kolpacki and dedicated in July of 1887. Much of the South Side population turned out for the ceremony. Community meetings, concerts,
theatrical performances, and dances were also held at Kosciuszko Hall,
which became the principal social and cultural center for South Side
Poles until it was torn down in the 1960s.

The Kosciuszko Guard inspired pride on the part of the Polish community, and its captains were community leaders. Sadly, the guard's first
mobilization ended in tragedy. In 1886 the unit was summoned, with
other guard groups, to quell labor unrest at the Bay View Rolling Mill,
which employed many Poles from St. Stanislaus parish. At the time,
Milwaukee had become a center of the nationwide movement for an
eight-hour workday. Two German labor leaders, Robert Schilling and
Paul Grottkau, organized the Eight-Hour League, which set a deadline
of May 1, 1886, for Milwaukee's employers to comply with its demands.
As the date drew near, strikes spread throughout the city, and when
the deadline arrived, more than six thousand men had left their places
of work. Many were Poles. On May 3, a general strike shut down the
entire city.

On May 4, about a thousand striking Polish laborers met at
St. Stanislaus Church to march on the last major industrial plant that
remained open — the Bay View Rolling Mill. As the crowd gathered
outside the plant, a delegation of labor leaders went inside to confer with
the plant's managers. Meanwhile, Governor Jeremiah Rusk had called
out three militia units, including the Kosciuszko Guard. As the guardsmen entered the gates of the rolling mill, the crowd pelted them with
sticks, stones, and garbage. The plant was shut down, but anticipating
further trouble, the guardsmen spent the night. On the morning of May
5, an even larger crowd, about fifteen hundred strong, assembled at
St. Stanislaus and marched again on the rolling mill. As they approached
the plant, the militia opened fire, killing somewhere between five and
nine people. Two of the dead were bystanders — a Polish schoolboy and
a retired Bay View man. Polish laborers filled St. Stanislaus Church for
the funerals of the slain. Outraged at the guard's participation in the
attack on their countrymen, Polish workers boycotted the businesses of
Kosciuszko Guard members. Afterward, however, the militia commander
was cleared of charges concerning his conduct, while Paul Grottkau and

several of the marchers were jailed. Some employers refused to hire Polish workers, and the eight-hour workday movement was dead.

The Kosciuszko Guard was mobilized several times after its disastrous participation in the Bay View disturbances. In 1898, at the beginning of the Spanish-American War, the Kosciuszko Guard was designated Company K of the First Wisconsin and sent to Florida, but the war ended before the company entered combat. Company K was called into service again briefly on the Mexican border in 1916. In 1917, the 250 enlisted men and six officers of Company K were called up for combat in the trenches of France during World War I. After the war, the company was reorganized as Company K of the 127th Infantry, Thirty-second Division, and saw action again in the Pacific theater during World War II.

ARTS AND CULTURE

In addition to the many fraternal benefit societies, a variety of performing arts groups reinforced Polish cultural identity through their meetings and public performances. Poles living under the Prussian partition had established their own versions of German singing societies and later carried the tradition to America. In Milwaukee, as in other Polish settlements, no official celebration was complete without a performance of religious, patriotic, and folk songs. Amateur choirs and singing groups also presented concerts in Polish churches, halls, and theaters. In 1873 Antoni Małłek, a recent immigrant from the Prussian partition, organized a choir at St. Stanislaus parish. His brother, Konstanty (Constantine) Małłek, subsequently served as organist and teacher at St. Stanislaus, St. Hyacinth, and St. Adalbert churches, and directed many Polish singing groups in Milwaukee. Early choir concerts were usually held in church halls, but the completion of Kosciuszko Hall in 1887 provided a venue for all kinds of musical and dramatic productions. About 1885, a group of music and drama lovers formed the Moniuszko Society, which later became the Harmonia Society. Harmonia was soon followed by a women's equivalent, the Kalina Society. For more than forty years, Harmonia and Kalina performed separately and together at Polish patriotic observances, produced several plays, and staged a large number of operettas. In the 1920s the Polish Opera Club even staged grand operas in the Polish language, including Stanisław Moniuszko's great national opera, *Halka*.

In the pretelevision age, amateur drama was another popular form of recreation for both audience and performers. Beginning in the 1880s, a number of Polish literary and dramatic societies took the stage in Milwaukee, as elsewhere around the country. Nearly every parish had its own theatrical group. Parish choirs sometimes performed dramatic pieces and operettas, in addition to concerts. Beginning about 1915, the Polish Theatre Organization presented local Polish actors performing drama and comedy in a converted movie house of the same name at Eighth and West Mitchell Streets. A later group, the Polish Fine Arts Club, originated with a performance of Polish dancing and singing called the "Polish Wedding" that was performed at an international festival held at Milwaukee's lakefront in the summer of 1930.

THE POLISH PRESS

Immigrants yearned for news from home and about their countrymen in other American communities. New arrivals also needed advice on adjusting to American society and politics. As educated Poles began arriving in the United States, they attempted to meet these needs by establishing newspapers written in the Polish language. After two Polish-language newspapers, Chicago's *Przyjaciel Ludu* (The People's Friend) and New York's *Zgoda* (Accord), were briefly published in Milwaukee at the start of the 1880s, an ambitious young immigrant named Michael Kruszka put Milwaukee on the map for Polish newspaper readers.

Michał (Michael) Kruszka (1860–1918) was the son of a relatively prosperous Polish farmer in Słabomierz, in the Poznań province of the Prussian partition of Poland. He received the equivalent of a high school education and showed an early inclination for both journalism and politics. In 1877 he was arrested for anti-Prussian activities but was released because he was not yet eighteen. In 1880 Kruszka left Poland for the United States, working in New York, New Jersey, and Chicago before arriving in Milwaukee in 1883. After two unsuccessful attempts to establish independent newspapers in Milwaukee, Kruszka launched the

Kuryer Polski (Polish Courier) on June 23, 1888, with one hundred twenty-five dollars borrowed from friends. He built the paper into America's first successful Polish-language daily, with a nationwide readership. Kruszka continued as editor of the influential newspaper until his death in 1918, when his son-in-law Stanislaus Zwierzchowski assumed the editorship. Three years later, Zwierzchowski turned management of the paper over to Czesław (Chester) Dziadulewicz, who served as editor until 1938.

Michael Kruszka was a controversial figure and an outspoken critic of Wisconsin's church hierarchy, especially Milwaukee's German archbishop, Sebastian Messmer. From the pages of the *Kuryer*, Kruszka advocated tirelessly for Polish clergy to be given a larger role, and especially for a Polish bishop to be appointed. He opposed the building of extravagant churches, since the resultant debt burden fell on working-class parishioners who could ill afford it. Kruszka also argued for introducing Polish-language instruction in public schools. The church viewed this as an attempt to undermine the parochial school system. As the disputes between the church hierarchy and the *Kuryer Polski* became increasingly bitter, Messmer attempted to counter the influence of the popular paper by supporting a series of newspapers that presented the church's point of view. In 1906 the Reverend Bolesław Góral, with church backing, established the *Nowiny Polskie* (The Polish News). Messmer subsequently issued a pastoral letter forbidding the faithful to read the *Kuryer*, on pain of forfeiting their right to church sacraments. Parish priests were directed to read the letter from the pulpit and to inquire into their parishioners' reading habits during confession. The pastoral interdiction had little effect on the *Kuryer*'s circulation, however, and the church-sanctioned *Nowiny* never matched the readership of the forbidden *Kuryer*.

Several other Wisconsin towns with large Polish populations launched their own publishing ventures. In 1891 Zygmunt Hutter and Teofil Krutza of Stevens Point began printing a farm weekly called *Rolnik* (The Farmer). Brothers Szczepan (Stephen) and Józef (Joseph) Worzalla purchased the newspaper in 1903. The paper continued to expand until 1929, after which sales declined steadily until *Rolnik* published its last issue in 1960. In 1908 the Worzalla brothers launched another Polish paper, *Gwiazda Polarna* (The Polar Star), which was aimed at a more urban audience than the *Rolnik* and soon outstripped it in circulation. Like other Polish presses, Worzalla Brothers published a variety of other printed matter, including books, schoolbooks, calendars, pictures, and other items.

SPORTS

Athletic activity was another arena reinforcing Polish American identity. Organized athletics began when the Polish Falcons introduced physical drills, weightlifting, and gymnastics to its members. The Falcons established two principal lodges, or "nests," in Milwaukee. One was located on the South Side and the other, still in existence, on the North Side. After the turn of the twentieth century, boxing and wrestling became popular spectator sports, and several Polish fighters from Milwaukee gained a measure of fame. Bowling also enjoyed widespread popularity among Milwaukee's Poles. Many neighborhood taverns, and even churches, had a few lanes, while local groups of the major fraternal organizations sponsored their own leagues.

Polish parishes and businesses also fielded their own teams to play the quintessentially American sport of baseball. Amateur teams played on makeshift fields and diamonds. In 1908 Louis Fons, a prominent real estate agent, built the South Side Ball Park, with capacity for five thousand spectators. A baseball player himself, Fons helped to organize a semiprofessional team that became known as the Kosciuszko Reds. The popular team played from 1909 until 1919 and won several championships in their distinctive red and white uniforms.

"WE, THE MILWAUKEE POLES"

By the early twentieth century, nearly half of Wisconsin's Poles lived in Milwaukee County — by far the largest concentration in the state. Jobs and social opportunities drew both newcomers and second-generation Poles whose families had settled in other parts of the state to Milwaukee. In urban areas, Polish immigrants who had grown up knowing only farm work were usually hired for unskilled industrial jobs. In Milwaukee, they worked in foundries, tanneries, breweries, and mills, or they graded streets and dug sewers. Later, they took up skilled trades, such as carpentry, and with time, they began to establish their own small businesses, including grocery stores and saloons. Polish women also contributed to the economy. Almost all single Polish women were employed. Some started out in domestic service, but a sizable number worked in factories or retail establishments. Even after marriage, many women continued to earn an income, if not working for wages, then by sewing, raising livestock, or taking in boarders.

By the turn of the twentieth century, several of Milwaukee's Poles had founded successful industrial enterprises. Casimir Janiszewski's Superior Steel Products Co., Sylvester Wabiszewski's Maynard Electric Steel Corp., and Miszewski and Bykowski's National Plating Co. employed many Polish laborers. Other Poles entered professions such as medicine, architecture, pharmacy, and law. One of Milwaukee's foremost Polish community leaders was Francis X. Swietlik, a Milwaukee-born Pole who received his law degree in 1914. After practicing law for twenty years, he became dean of the Marquette University law school in 1934. In Polish circles, Swietlik attained national stature as *cenzor* of the Polish National Alliance, one of the organization's highest offices.

As Poles increased in numbers and gained confidence in American society, they began to enter public life. In Milwaukee, August Rudziński was elected to the county board in 1878. His son, Theodore Rudziński, became an alderman in 1882. While still at a disadvantage in the overwhelmingly German city of Milwaukee, Poles formed a sizable voting bloc within the Democratic Party. Depending on the issue, however, they did not always vote Democratic, and since Polish voters often held the balance of power, neither party could afford to disregard them. Between five and eight of the city's wards sent Polish Americans to the city council, and Poles held a number of municipal offices. For example, Ignace Czerwinski was the first Polish American member of the board of fire and police commissioners. Frank Niezorawski served on the board of public works from 1900 to 1904 and was succeeded by Stanley E. Czerwinski. In 1927 Leon M. Gurda became Milwaukee's second building inspector and served for many years. Walter J. Swietlik was the first Polish American commissioner of public works. Roman Czerwinski served as city comptroller from 1890 to 1894, and for the next forty years, Polish Americans had a virtual corner on the post.

From the mid-1880s on, Poles moved into more prominent offices. Francis Borchardt was elected to the Wisconsin state assembly in 1882, and newspaper editor Michael Kruszka became a state senator in 1893. A steady stream of Polish lawmakers followed them to Madison. In the twentieth century, Wisconsin's Polish voters sent five of their own to the United States Congress. John C. Kleczka of Milwaukee served two terms in the U.S. House of Representatives (1919–1923). Thaddeus F. Wasielewski, also of Milwaukee, served three terms in the House (1941–1947). State senator Clement J. Zablocki was elected to seventeen terms beginning in 1949. He was succeeded by Gerald D. Kleczka, who served from April 1984 until January 2004. Besides the four Democrats from Milwaukee, Alvin E. O'Konski (originally Okonski), who was born near Kewaunee, Wisconsin, served fifteen terms in the House of Representatives (1943–1973) as a Republican from Rhinelander.

POLONIA REBORN

During World War I, immigration from Poland came to a halt, but, harboring hope that the defeat of Prussia could result in the liberation of Poland, Polish Americans took a keen interest in the war's progress. A number of young Polish American men enlisted in the armed forces with the goal of freeing Poland. Under the slogan, "He who buys a bond helps Poland," many Polish Americans bought liberty bonds to aid the war effort. After the end of hostilities, there was a brief resurgence of immigration, but U.S. restrictions imposed in 1919 virtually cut off the flow. At the same time, with Polish nationhood restored by the Treaty of Versailles, a much-publicized campaign encouraged Poles living in America to move back to Poland in order to help rebuild the nation. Some immigrants did return to Poland, whether for patriotic reasons or because they were homesick and had not become successful in America, but the numbers were not large. The period between the two world wars nevertheless inspired resurgent patriotism among Poles on both sides of the Atlantic. Polish Americans followed news of their homeland closely, and many contributed financial resources to bolster the growth of the reborn nation.

Poland's independence was short-lived, however. Within days of Hitler's attack on Poland in September 1939, Milwaukee's Polish community mobilized to provide their countrymen with humanitarian aid. Polish American organizations and community leaders formed the Polish Relief Committee, which later became Wisconsin Chapter No. 18 of a national organization, American Relief for Poland. The relief committee was headed by Milwaukee's most prominent Polish Americans: Attorney Thaddeus Wasielewski was the first president. He was succeeded by Leon M. Gurda, Milwaukee's building inspector, while Judge John C. Kleczka served as honorary president. Francis X. Swietlik, dean of Marquette University's School of Law, was elected as the national president of American Relief for Poland.

POSTWAR POLONIA

World War II represented a watershed for Wisconsin's Polish community. After the war's end, the population boom brought on by returning GIs, coupled with rapid economic growth, caused many Polish families in Milwaukee to move out of the old neighborhoods into newly developed suburbs. Since new immigration had for the most part ended a generation before, Wisconsin's Poles were largely assimilated to American culture. Polish parishes and other organizations made the inevitable transition from the Polish to the English language.

After the end of the war in Europe, many Polish military men and civilians found themselves outside of Poland and unable to return because of the hostile Communist government. In 1948 Polish Americans in Milwaukee organized the Committee for the Resettlement of Poles in Wisconsin. The committee issued affidavits of support for displaced persons living in German refugee camps and in England. It also organized English-language courses for the new immigrants and helped them find jobs and housing. Before long, about five hundred families had settled in the Milwaukee area. Most were sponsored and employed by the Patrick Cudahy firm. Patrick Cudahy's brother, John Cudahy, had been the American ambassador to Poland during the interwar years.

Despite the efforts of Polish Americans to assist the postwar immigrants in adjusting to American life, the different backgrounds and expectations of the two groups stood in the way of easy integration.

Polish Americans assumed that the newcomers would depend on them for advice and material assistance, much as they or their parents and grandparents had depended on those who came before. The refugees, however, sometimes looked down on their would-be benefactors and disparaged their ignorance of Polish language and culture, as well as their blue-collar status. Many postwar immigrants were disappointed to find that their Polish education and professional skills were not always valued in the United States. Rather than joining the established Polonian institutions, they founded their own organizations, often with a military or cultural focus. In Milwaukee, these included the Polish Combatants' Association (1952), the Polonia Sport Club (1950), and Polanki, the Polish Women's Cultural Club of Milwaukee (1953), as well as others that no longer exist. A Wisconsin chapter of the Polish American Congress, a national political action organization formed in the aftermath of World War II, also emerged during this period.

For most of the Cold War years, the Polish government made it difficult for Polish citizens to travel abroad, much less emigrate. With the rise of the Solidarity trade union in 1980, passport regulations were temporarily liberalized and a number of Poles, mainly well-educated professionals, took advantage of the opportunity to leave Poland. After the imposition of martial law in December 1981, the Polish government even forced some jailed Solidarity activists to emigrate as a condition of their release. With the re-establishment of democratic government in Poland in the 1990s, it became easier for Poles to travel abroad. The economic dislocation that accompanied freedom meant high unemployment and low wages, which led many Poles to seek better opportunities elsewhere. Since Poland's entry to the European Union, however, and because of the weakened U.S. economy, fewer Poles have been coming to the United States, and some are returning to Poland.

The years after World War II have seen major changes in Wisconsin's Polish American community. As the descendants of Polish immigrants abandoned the old neighborhoods for the suburbs, new immigrants, mainly from Latin America, have moved into the former Polish areas. Polish parishes have lost their ethnic identity due to population shifts and mergers with non-Polish parishes. Descendants of Polish immigrants became integrated into mainstream American society, and membership in older Polish fraternal societies declined. A number of Polish organizations dissolved or merged with each other, and Poles seemed to be on track to lose much of their distinctiveness in the all-American melting pot.

The "Roots" movement of the 1970s sparked a resurgence of ethnic pride across the nation, which touched many assimilated Polish Americans as well. The election of Polish cardinal Karol Wojtyła to the papacy in 1978 and the founding of the Solidarity trade union in 1980 focused world attention on Poland and stimulated interest in Polish affairs. A group of Milwaukee Polish Americans founded the Syrena Polish Folk Dance Ensemble in 1977. In Madison, a Polish Heritage Club was formed in 1979. Milwaukee launched an annual Polish Fest in 1982, as one of several large ethnic festivals held at the city's lakefront festival park. Wisconsin Dells initiated a Polish Fest in 1990, and Armstrong Creek held its first annual Polish Heritage Day celebration in 1991. Stevens Point's Polish Heritage Awareness Society of Central Wisconsin, founded in 1992, and the Polish Heritage Society of Northeastern Wisconsin in Green Bay are two more organizations that explicitly strive to preserve Polish culture and heritage.

INTO THE FUTURE

Renewed Polish immigration during the 1980s and 1990s added new layers on top of the old Polish community. The newer immigrants were generally well educated and adapted easily to American society. They might converse with each other in Polish, but most of them also spoke English. Nevertheless, like early Polish immigrants attending German or Irish churches, Polish-born Catholics in Milwaukee on the cusp of the twenty-first century wanted to worship in their native language. In a pattern reminiscent of the past, Polish-speaking Catholics first attended Polish-language services conducted by a visiting priest, then formed a committee and appealed to the Archbishop for permission to organize a separate parish. In 2003, they created a Polish-speaking congregation, which shares the old Polish church of SS Cyril and Methodius with its now English-speaking congregation. The new Polish parish was named for St. Maximilian Kolbe, a Polish priest who was martyred in Auschwitz and canonized by Pope John Paul II in 1982. Then, in January of 2010, the installation of Jerome Listecki as Archbishop of Milwaukee brought belated fulfillment to the old aspirations of Milwaukee's Polish Catholics for a bishop who shares their ethnic heritage.

In 2000, Milwaukee's Polish American community achieved another milestone when the Polish Fest organization dedicated its own building, known as the Polish Center of Wisconsin. Keeping pace with changing times, the founders followed the path of postwar migration and purchased property in the southwestern suburb of Franklin, rather than in the traditional Polish neighborhood. Significantly, the Polish Center's parklike setting and architectural style hark back to the manor houses of the landed gentry, not the modest cottages Polish peasants would have lived in.

In the twenty-first century, when the descendants of immigrants have successfully entered the mainstream of American life, the challenge will be to maintain a sense of Polish identity. It may help to look back — to recall the culture their ancestors left in Poland, the values they brought to Wisconsin, and the hardships they overcame to build a better life for themselves and their heirs.

Mother and child in front of their cottage near Windlake Avenue on Milwaukee's South Side, ca. 1885. Many Polish immigrant families realized their dreams of home ownership in worker's cottages like this, built on cedar post foundations. After some years, the house would be jacked up and "underpinned" with a brick basement. Often, the basements were built high enough to accommodate separate living quarters. The result has come to be known as a "Polish flat."

WHi Image ID 87499

Historic Photo Collection / Milwaukee Public Library

Pulaski Street, in Milwaukee's East Side Polish neighborhood, followed the crooked path of a filled-in ravine. The store at left was John Fojut's grocery, 952 Pulaski Street (now 1870 North Pulaski Street), 1922.

WHi Image ID 88696

Joseph B. Kuszewski's grocery at 951 Bremen Street (now 2541 North Bremen Street), ca. 1905. The Kuszewski family lived above the store. *Below*: The interior of Paul Kuszewski's grocery at the same location, ca. 1910. Paul was the son of Joseph B. Kuszewski.

WHi Image ID 88695

Bernard Kosciesza (behind counter, center) opened this meat market at 788 Forest Home Avenue (now 1583 West Forest Home Avenue) in Milwaukee around 1916. Various types of sausage hang from overhead racks, with other smoked meats on the right.

WHi Image ID 88693

Wedding portrait and certificate of naturalization for Sylvester Gurda, dated July 10, 1888. Sylvester Gurda worked as a letter carrier in Milwaukee. He married Victoria Orzechowski on September 7, 1886. Two of their sons became architects: Leon was Milwaukee's Building Inspector, and Francis designed St. Adalbert's Church in Milwaukee.

Certificate of Naturalization

Be it Remembered, That at the Municipal Court, held at Milwaukee, for the County of Milwaukee, in the State of Wisconsin, in the United States of America, on the _Tenth_ day of _July_ in the year of Our Lord One Thousand Eight Hundred and Eighty _Eight_ _Sylvester Gurda_ a native of _Germany_ exhibited a Petition praying to be admitted to become a CITIZEN OF THE UNITED STATES, and it appearing to the said Court that he had declared on Oath before the _Municipal_ Court for the _City & County_ of _Milwaukee State_ of _Wisconsin_ on the _19th_ day of _October_ A. D. 18_80_, that it was bona-fide his intention to become a Citizen of the United States, and to RENOUNCE FOREVER all allegiance and fidelity to any Foreign Prince, Potentate, State or Sovereignty whatsoever, and particularly to _William I German Emperor_ of whom he was at that time a subject; and the said _Sylvester Gurda_ having on his solemn Oath declared, and also made proof thereof, by competent testimony of _Francis S Frame & Robt W Davidson_ citizens of the United States, that he had resided one year and upwards in the State of Wisconsin, and within the United States of America upwards of five years immediately preceding his application; and it appearing to the satisfaction of the Court that during that time he had behaved as a man of good moral character, attached to the principles of the Constitution of the United States, and well disposed to the good order and happiness of the same; and having on his solemn oath declared before the same Court that he would support the Constitution of the United States, and that he did absolutely and entirely renounce and abjure all allegiance and fidelity to every Foreign Prince, Potentate, State and Sovereignty whatsoever, and particularly to _William II German Emperor_ of whom he was before a subject.

THEREUPON THE COURT admitted the said _Sylvester Gurda_ to become a Citizen of the United States, and ordered all proceedings aforesaid to be recorded by the Clerk of the said Court; and which was done accordingly.

IN WITNESS WHEREOF, I have hereunto affixed my hand and the seal of the Municipal Court, at Milwaukee, this _10th_ day of _July_ in the year One Thousand Eight Hundred and Eighty _Eight_ and of the Independence of the United States of America, the One Hundred and _thirtenth_

Julius Heiswinkel
Clerk of the Municipal Court.

St. Stanislaus (1866) was
the first Polish parish in
Milwaukee and the first
urban Polish parish in
the United States. The
first church was a small
building purchased from
a Lutheran congrega-
tion. This is the second
church building, dedi-
cated in 1873 and photo-
graphed by the Historic
American Buildings Sur-
vey in 1960.

Below: Interior of St.
Stanislaus Church, fac-
ing the altar, 1960

Historic Photo Collection / Milwaukee Public Library

Historic Photo Collection / Milwaukee Public Library

An expanding population of Polish immigrants on Milwaukee's South Side meant that St. Stanislaus Church could no longer accommodate all of its faithful. In 1882, under the leadership of the Rev. Hyacinth Gulski, the congregation decided to divide the parish's territory and establish a new congregation, St. Hyacinth's, for parishioners living west of 5th Avenue (present-day South 10th Street). The church was dedicated in 1883.

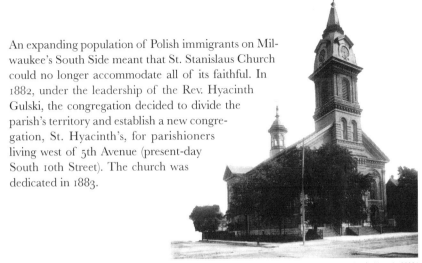

Kwasniewski Photographs, UW- Milwaukee Libraries-Archives, kw00024

Kwasniewski Photographs, UW-Milwaukee Libraries, Archives, kw00020

St. Josaphat Basilica stands on Lincoln Avenue in the heart of Milwaukee's South Side Polish neighborhood. Modeled after St. Peter's in Rome, St. Josaphat's is the largest church in Milwaukee. It was completed in 1901 and designated a basilica in 1929. The smaller building to the left was the real estate office of Barney Czerwinski when this photo was taken, ca. 1920.

Milwaukee County Historical Society

Kwasniewski Photographs , UW-Milwaukee Libraries-Archives, 15316

Portrait of Michael Kruszka in 1912. Kruszka founded the daily *Kuryer Polski* (Polish Courier) in 1888 and served as editor until his death in 1918.

The Reverend Wacław (Wenceslaus) Kruszka, half-brother of Michael Kruszka. As pastor of St. Wenceslaus Church in Ripon and St. Adalbert Church in Milwaukee, Kruszka agitated for the appointment of Polish bishops. He wrote a pioneering history of Polish settlement in America.

Kaszubian fishermen from the Hel peninsula in Poland settled this strip of low-lying land known as Jones Island in the Milwaukee Harbor. Ca. 1890.

Fishing shanties and boats on Jones Island. Most of the island's inhabitants made their living by fishing and related trades.

Bronze statue of Tadeusz Kościuszko, erected in Kosciuszko Park, Milwaukee, and sculpted by Gaetano Trentanove. The *Milwaukee Journal* reported that sixty thousand people attended the dedication of the Kosciuszko Monument in 1905.

WHi Image ID 53753

Kwasniewski Photographs, UW-Milwaukee Libraries-Archives, kw000835

Company K of the Wisconsin National Guard, popularly known as the Kosciuszko Guard, was mustered into federal service for World War I at Camp Douglas on July 31, 1917.

Kwasniewski Photographs, UW-Milwaukee Libraries-Archives, A00866

Polish children display American patriotism at this picnic sponsored by the Dąbrówka women's society on July 11, 1912, in Milwaukee.

Kwasniewski Photographs, UW-Milwaukee Libraries-Archives, A9045

Amateur dramatics were a popular form of entertainment in the pretelevision age. This group of actors from the Amateur Dramatic Circle of St. Hyacinth's Church don costumes depicting Polish and military characters for a 1914 performance.

Thomas Hajewski

Maciej Wojda (first row, center) stands next to his wife, Ewa, who holds their youngest son, Tadeusz, in front of their house on First Avenue in the Town of Lake (now South 6th Street in Milwaukee). The occasion was the wedding of Maciej and Ewa's oldest daughter, Franciska (Frania) to Stanisław Śliżewski on August 8, 1898.

MEMOIR OF MY LIFE

Maciej Wojda, November 1928

Translated from the original Polish by
Michael J. Mikoś and Susan Gibson Mikoś

HEADNOTE

Maciej (Mathias or Matthew) Wojda (1853–1933) came to Milwaukee in 1868, just two years after the founding of the city's first Polish parish — St. Stanislaus. His life story is representative of many early Polish immigrant experiences. Two of his older brothers had arrived earlier to find work and buy passage for the rest of the family. Maciej and his family entered the United States through the port of Quebec. Maciej's father, Paweł (Paul), worked in Milwaukee for a short time, then found work on a farm in Muskego and soon purchased his own farm. After Paweł died, the family moved back to Milwaukee. As a young man, Maciej worked briefly in Michigan and Chicago, but he returned to Milwaukee and learned carpentry under a German builder, John Fellens. He worked on construction projects in various cities, including Milwaukee, St. Francis, Fond du Lac, and Madison. Later, he and his brother Piotr went into business together.

In 1928 Maciej decided to write a memoir of his life. He divided the 160-page manuscript into three parts. The first part introduces his parents and sketches the life histories of his eight siblings. The second part describes his life in Poland, the journey to America, and his life in Wisconsin. In the third part—which is not included in this excerpt—Maciej reviews his career as a carpenter and builder, then offers observations and anecdotes relating to various subjects, including drinking, medical care, Milwaukee priests, religious fanaticism, American Indians, and the number thirteen.

Maciej addressed this memoir to his children and grandchildren. Although he had little formal schooling, Maciej was a shrewd and articulate observer whose descriptions of women and minority communities reflect the time period in which he lived and the beliefs he held. His spontaneous writing style gives readers a sense of what life was like in the early twentieth century.

The original manuscript of Maciej Wojda's memoir, written in Polish, was donated to the Polish Roman Catholic Union in 1943 by Jan Rąpała, editor of the Polish Roman Catholic newspaper *Nowiny Polskie*. The handwritten document is now housed in the archives of the Polish Museum of America in Chicago.

TRANSLATORS' NOTE

The language of the memoir reflects the speech of nineteenth-century Polish peasants. Maciej's wit and lively intelligence are also evident in his colorful, sometimes idiosyncratic turns of phrase. Like other Polish immigrants from the Prussian partition, Maciej spoke German almost as well as he spoke Polish, and he uses German freely (with Polish orthography) when recalling German conversations. He also mixes in occasional English words and phrases, even though he criticizes this practice in the younger generation of Polish Americans. Maciej's English words are indicated in this text by the use of italics.

The portion of Maciej's memoir presented here includes the bulk of parts 1 and 2. Because of space limitations, some passages have been omitted; deletions are indicated with bracketed ellipses. In translating Maciej's memoir, we have tried to preserve the essence of his narrative style. For the sake of clarity, we have introduced standard punctuation and spelling of English words and proper nouns. We have also broken up long sentences, a change that is not indicated by ellipses.

MY FAMILY IN THE OLD COUNTRY
AND HERE IN AMERICA

I, Maciej Wojda, a Polish old-timer, a citizen of the United States of North America, residing at present in the city of Milwaukee, state of Wisconsin, in the parish of St. Josaphat, now in my eighties, after my experiences in life, want to leave to my children, grandchildren, and great-grandchildren this memoir, so it may serve for instruction and meditation. [...]

I was born in Poland, in the village of Falmierowo, and baptized in Gromadno on the twenty-eighth of May in 1853. I am the son of Paweł and Joanna, née Mulka, Wojda, who came from Frydląd [now Debrzno] near Złotów. There were six of us brothers and three sisters, that is*:

1. Jan
2. Piotr
3. Michał
4. Józef
5. Maryanna
6. Paweł
7. Maciej
8. Paulina
9. Ewa

Jan, the oldest, [was] a wheelwright because Father was a wheelwright. Jan was a Prussian soldier and took part in two wars, in Denmark and Austria, and was already married with two children.

Piotr was also a wheelwright and a Prussian soldier, but he wasn't in any war because he finished his service in 1865. At the beginning of 1866 he went to America with our brother Michał, who was a tailor but was not in the military. Two days after Piotr's departure, three summonses came for him to report for service: one at noon, the second in the evening, and the third at midnight, and then they telegraphed to Bremen to stop him but the ship was already too far out at sea, so they had to leave him in peace, thanks be to God, because on account of that, Willy [King Wilhelm I of Prussia] had one less Polish soldier in the war. Before [Piotr] went away, he had a lot of trouble getting a permit to leave, and if he had come across a tough Kraut, who knows if he wouldn't have had to go to war, but he came out all right because he happened on a good man, though a German, and [he had] an even better wife. When he went to the sergeant in Wyrzysk for a travel permit, he had big problems, since war was already in the air. He was questioned about where he was going and where he would be in a year, because he could only get a pass for a year. But his wife answered in German: "Oh, my dear man, how can a man know exactly where he is going to live and work? Your Honor, just write, 'In New York.'" And he: "You are quite right, my dear madam," and he wrote, "New York." And you can see from this that even among Germans there are good people, but very few, it's more than certain.

* In the original, this list appears before the start of the memoir.

And my brothers went to New York and from there to Buffalo and they were there for a year. My brother Michał got a job with a tailor, and my brother Piotr worked in a tannery, and after a year they came to Milwaukee. My brother completely forgot about Willy, since he developed a short memory then, which can happen to anyone, and he thought to himself, "You can go fly a kite, you little Germans, because three years of service for free is enough!"

I came here to Milwaukee with my parents, with their help, in 1868.

My brother Michał, a tailor, was short and a very good-natured man. He got married here in Milwaukee, it seems to me in 1869, to Józefina Bachert. Their children live here in Milwaukee. My brother Piotr also got married here and his children live here. His wife is still living, and we buried Michał's widow on October 22, 1928, since my brothers died a long time ago.

My brother Józef, a blacksmith, also got married here in Milwaukee, and he died in Michigan on a *farm* in Posen. His children live somewhere there but I don't know them. He was almost the strongest one in the whole family and was somewhat vengeful; he wouldn't forgive anyone who insulted him. He was also a Prussian soldier, and the Austrian war almost took him by surprise as a recruit, since he was conscripted in the fall and the war broke out in spring, so he took part in it in 1866. He served in Kolberg in the Fifty-fourth, in the Eighth Company. My brother Jan was also a soldier in the same regiment, only in the Second Company. My brother Piotr had a black belt; he was in the Thirty-fourth Regiment and he was close to the French border, but all of them were in the infantry. After the war, Józef was transferred to Harburg, which was taken from the Austrians after the war; he was in the Seventy-first Regiment there. It was on this account that we went to America by way of Hamburg, so we could say good-bye to him, because Hamburg is just across the canal from Harburg. I went to get him with Father and Jan, and he got leave for two days, from Friday to Sunday night. [...] [Józef] still had to serve some six months until he had served out his three years there, too. [Then] Father sent him the passage to America and it was high time because the vengeful Prussian [Wilhelm I] was again getting ready for war with France, and if he had not had a free passage, who knows if he would have made it to America. He would have had to fight again for someone else's sins, and perhaps die, not by his own choice but by force, because the Kaiser wanted it so.

My sister Maryanna enjoyed America the least, because some three months after our arrival in Milwaukee she died at my brother Jan's on Buffalo Street near Lake Michigan. She was a servant for some people, and we were already on the *farm* in Franklin, now St. Martins. She was supposed to get married soon, to Michał Bąk, her fiancé, who came to America with us. Several months later he died, too, of heartbreak for her, from consumption. [...] She was a girl the likes of which there are few in the world—a good, mild, pretty, healthy, and strong girl. She never said a bad word to anyone and everybody who knew her liked her, and she was the lead girl in the harvest every summer.

My brother Paweł is still living and is a retired American soldier. He collects a pension and lives in Edmond, Oklahoma. He, for sure, had the most stormy life out of our whole family, because even in the old country he was full of what people call "to eat and drink well and do little work." While he was still a little boy he was taken on as a servant at the manor in Izabela, to the Count and Countess Koczorowski, and there he found a very good teacher in the person of Jan Badziński. He was, it seems to me, the most contrary servant in the entire Duchy of Poznań. Not that he would harm anyone, not at all, but he would surely make mischief wherever he could, with the greatest pleasure, and then he was not guilty because he would blame someone else, and then later he would laugh to his heart's content because he had made mischief for someone. But aside from that he was a good man—nice and helpful, and it is known that the servant is like his master. And when we came to America he thought it would be the same, but here it didn't work. There was a saying here then: "If you want to eat and live, then work," but he didn't like that, so in 1872 after that great fire in Chicago he joined the United States Army. (I who am writing this also wanted to, but they chased me away because I was still too young, just a stripling.) Paweł was admitted to the cavalry, the Fifth Regiment, under General Crook. [...] and he saw action in the Black Hills, in the battle of 1876 where General Custer perished with his entire regiment. [...]

When my brother Paweł had served his four years he came to Milwaukee, to us, with six hundred dollars, but it didn't last very long because it came easily and went even more easily, and again poverty, and no thought of work. So he joined the army again and stayed there until he had served out his thirty years, and now he is a veteran and collects a pension under the false name George Snider, and lives in Oklahoma.

There he married a Polish woman who is supposed to come from Biał-ośliwie, and they had two sons and one daughter. The railroad killed one son. I didn't see Paweł for some thirty-five years, and some fifteen years ago he came here on a visit, but I didn't recognize him. He stayed here only a couple of days and went away as he had come, and I wouldn't recognize him today. I do know his son, Frank, because he was here some six months. He had good schooling. He is a teacher and a good man and a Catholic. He speaks Polish poorly but he understands everything. He is still a bachelor, though he is already over thirty. Enough about him.

[Next] comes this wise guy who is writing this [Maciej], but we'll leave him in peace and I'll save him for the very end because he will get the most, only no one should think it will be praise, far from it, because he made the most mischief and tempted good and evil.

Next, my sister Paulina. She was a very quiet woman. She was never angry with anyone, [and] forgave everyone. She had a good word for everyone and in return everyone also liked and respected her. She never liked to quarrel, and if someone tried to convince her that black was white, she would say he was right for the sake of agreement, but she would think to herself, "Much you know! Why should I waste my breath quarreling with you?" She lived in Chicago almost from the time she was a little girl. Right after the Great Fire, she got married there to Ludwik Dorszewski, younger brother of Father Dorszewski, who held a high office in the Gniezno region since he was an administrator there. They brought up six children, three sons and three daughters. The oldest, Rozalja, died while still unmarried, and one son, Antoni, was shot to death at a young age. Two sons and two daughters live there permanently, because their parents died several years ago. The older, Franciszek, has been working in the same place since he was a little boy, for more than thirty years already, and for several years he has been a foreman. And the younger, Ludwik, is a pharmacist. He has his own pharmacy, from his brother-in-law, Mr. Ed Wolta, who died of influenza several years ago. His wife — the older sister, Maryanna—is a widow to this day and lives at 1641 Austin Boulevard, Cicero, Ill[inois], in her own new *bungalow* with her two sons, Ed and Teodor, who attend high school. The younger [sister], Paulina, keeps house for both brothers in the home their parents left them, because all three are still single, though by law they should have been married a long time ago. [...] Their parents died, that is, my sister

Paulina on May 15, 1927, and my brother-in-law, Ludwik, on August 18 of the same year—grant them eternal rest, oh Lord.

Now the last, my sister Ewa Hassa. She was four when we came to America. She married Jan, and they brought up six children: two sons and four daughters. [Jan] was a good and wise man and a resourceful head of the household, but misfortune had it that a city tramway killed their oldest son some eighteen years ago. He was just about to get married, and it hit his father very hard. [Jan] was already sickly, and that finished him off completely. Soon afterward, he passed away, too, but he left his wife a nice property: a brick *flat* with no debt, and she lives peacefully and runs the home with two of her daughters, because her son and her other two daughters are already married. She is a very calm and quiet woman (almost too quiet) and a very good housewife. She doesn't like gossip so she doesn't have many cronies and doesn't go anywhere without a good reason, but she takes care of her household exemplarily and skillfully. And that is more or less everything about my siblings.

MY LIFE IN THE OLD COUNTRY
AND HERE IN AMERICA

And now comes the one whose crony and school friend, the late Mrs. Łabęcka, née Miss Józefina Sikora, called "you hothead," that is I, Maciej Wojda.

Here I will describe the history of my life as accurately as possible, but I beg of you, please do not laugh at my writing or criticize it, because I didn't attend any high school, only a village school, and that not even regularly, since when there was work in the fields, it was "March!" whether you were a whippersnapper, a laborer, or a craftsman. And there was always a lot of it, leading the horses for plowing potatoes or beets, or during the harvest, pulling the horses up when grain was loaded onto wagons. Not like it is now when seventeen-year-old beanpoles still go to school with books under their arms, and they don't apply themselves to learning, but just chase girls. For the most part they'll end up neither fish nor fowl—too dumb for a good position and too lazy for honest, hard work. [...]

So then, as has already been written in the first chapter, I was born in 1853 in Falmierowo, Wyrzysk district, Bydgoszcz area, in the Duchy of Poznań, so I am a Poznań man, body and soul, and I will remain so until my death, and above all a Pole. Nevertheless, I can speak, not badly, four languages, that is: Polish, English, German, and as they say, *Low Dutch*, and in Dutch I could get by (but about that later, because one shouldn't mix everything up like peas and cabbage). Thus, I am not so dumb as some think, but if I don't know where to put a period or a comma in writing, it isn't my fault, because I didn't study that. That is for those who attend high school, but not for those who go to a village school. Because there has to be time for everything, and most of all for good learning, and I didn't have that; and therefore, I ask whoever reads this to have mercy on me and think to himself, "This poor fellow wanted to [study] but couldn't, while there are so many who can, but don't feel like it!"

My first school was in Gleśno near Wyrzysk, I don't remember for how long, because we lived on the Bagdad manorial farm, which belonged to Gleśno but was rented out. We lived there seven years, I know, and in 1864 we moved to Izabela. The closest town was Mrocza, in Zabartowo Parish. Count Kazimierz Koczorowski was the squire and he was a very good master. He didn't mistreat anyone and did not permit his officials to do so, under severe penalty. His greatest [show of] anger, when someone was guilty, was to say: "You dumbbell!" — and sometimes he would repeat it. On the other hand he had a wife who was a hard woman, because she was, after all, the Right Honorable Lady, née Princess Marinia Czartoryski. She was evil, and she swore until the palace was lit up with thunderbolts, which I heard with my own ears, because I was there almost every day after school, since my older brother Paweł was a servant there. I had it good there, because the masters had only one son, Józef, and he was almost the same age as I, so I got all his old clothes, and the servant liked me, because I did everything he demanded, and that was very often. [...]

When we moved there to Izabela (and it was right on Good Friday), there was a woman who taught — the widow Rąkowa. There wasn't much by way of learning, because she didn't know much herself, just enough to keep the children in a group, so they wouldn't run all over the village and make mischief, but not for long. Soon the teacher Kawczyński arrived and after him Bartkowski. [They were] both bachelors, and one

[was] worse than the other because they beat [us] like devils, and most often me, not because of learning, not at all, because I wasn't too dumb in learning, and I would have been still better if I had applied myself. But someone was behind me, tempting me, and to my misfortune, I was involved in every mischief, and at the end it got to the point where I was not even questioned, but if there was any complaint, then it was, "Wojda, come here!" and then, "March to your place and sit down." But what to sit on, because on what a man sits I couldn't, since it hurt too much, and it was not possible to stand because I had to sit down, but on my sides, and it hurt like the devil because for sure there were welts as long as snakes. [...]

Our village, Izabela, was a very joyful village and in a very nice location. It was right next to a beautiful little forest, like a park, the same as Second Avenue [next] to Kosciuszko Park — only there was no monument there. [...] We lived there four years, and if our brothers had not sent us our passage to America, my father wouldn't even have thought of moving, because my father had it good there. The squire liked and respected him very much. He would often go to my father in his workshop and always talked with him for a long while. When my father went to tell him that we were going to America, the master said: "What do you want there, Paweł? You have it good here with me. After all, I don't do you any harm. Over there, there is no milk and honey either. But too bad; if it cannot be otherwise, then go, but remember, if you don't like it there, come back and your place will be open for you." The master liked Father very much, since my father was a very sober, solid man. But he didn't like lies and flattery. [...] I never saw my father drunk, because he never went to the tavern.

Mother was a beloved mother, good [and] resourceful. We were never without bread — not any white nobles' bread, but the so-called once-sifted type. Mother was one of those housewives who say, "By the cat's measure it will last longer," and not, "Mother, fry as much as you have and when it's gone, we'll do without." Mother came from those regions they call Yellow Legs. Because she often used the German language, and when I was a little boy, I blabbered half in Polish and half in German. [...] Our father loved our mother and us very much, but he was stern and kept us firmly in hand. He didn't beat us often, but when he whacked us sometimes our ribs were creaking. When Mother beat us he didn't interfere; he would only say, "Well, you will give it to him, but do not kill him perchance," to which Mother would say, "Now this one got it." […]

Once I made my father very angry, for which I cannot forgive myself to this day, because I cut all the buttons off his overcoat. They were good military ones, yellow, with tabs. I bent them, and for that I had not only shame but great pain. I went to the alcove to sleep, but how could I sleep when the pain wouldn't let me? I didn't sleep the whole night, but was just turning from side to side. My father and mother slept in the living room, and they thought I was asleep already, but I heard every word of how my father complained to my mother:

"Joanna, probably nothing will come of this gallows bird."

And my mother begged my father, "But Paweł, please be quiet. He might still grow up to be the best boy, because he is good-natured and does everything I tell him to. He is mischievous, it's true, but when he comes to his senses he will be better."

And Father: "May God grant, but I do not believe it."

And my beloved mother spoke the truth, because from that time on I avoided mischief as much as I could, since it bothered me awfully that I had upset such a good father so much. Our father was short with a blond mustache, almost the same as I, only he wasn't such a bungler and he couldn't tell tall tales as I can, that's for sure, and my mother was slightly shorter, blond, small, with a round face and as nimble as a sixteen-year-old young lady. Father never smoked, but he took snuff quite a lot.

I finished school there and went to my First Holy Communion in 1867 on the day of Pentecost, and for the second time when we were going to America, in Zabartowo at Easter, 1868.

And now, my dear, to America! […]

Now we are going to America, the twenty-fifth of March, 1868. And we are going from Izabela by wagon to Białośliwie, since Uncle Paweł Mulka, Mother's brother, lived there. We were there for two days, and we left from there by train in the evening, and in the morning we were in Berlin. From Berlin we went to Hamburg; we stayed there for three days, [because] as you already know from the first chapter, my brother Józef served in the military there. We said good-bye to him because he stayed with us all three days, from Friday to Sunday evening. We boarded the ship on Monday morning, and it was a big sailing boat, the *Gutenberg*, entirely of iron. It had carried grain before, and now, for the first time, people.

It took us to Quebec, Canada. We traveled nine weeks and two days across the water. Once, there was such a violent storm that they locked us in the cabins and didn't let us out until morning, and then a terrible sight presented itself to us. One mast was broken, the front tip was missing, three sailors fell from the masts and drowned, one was killed, and the captain himself didn't know where we were, but the carpenters were already busy with repairs.

At the end we were only getting half a portion of food and almost no water, although we were rocking on it, and that was the greatest misery. On our ship, fifty-four people died, and when we reached land they didn't let us go into the city, but the ship stood out at sea, and tugs took us to an island because they thought there was a contagious sickness on the ship. They held us there for two weeks, and then, so no one would die, they let us out, wherever we wanted to go, except that they wouldn't let us into the city. The tugs took us to where the train was waiting, and [so we started] the journey into the world. And the cars were lousy, since the seats were just nailed together from boards, very hard, like rock, and the trains were dragging along like flies in tar, and on Sunday they took a holiday.

The first large city was Montreal, the second Berlin [now Kitchener, Ontario]. We also went near the waterfall [most likely Niagara] but from afar, until we dragged into Port Huron, and there again onto a ship, until finally [we came] to Milwaukee. Here my brothers already had an apartment rented for us for some two months, and they were starting to doubt that they would ever see us. That house still stands today at First and Greenfield Avenue, at that time Railroad Street. That house was almost the last one on the South Side, opposite where Kosciuszko Hall stands today. Józef Budka had a little house, and Malczewski, the father of Antek, the stonecutter who makes monuments opposite the Polish cemetery, lived there on Greenbush Street. They worked as well diggers and also had one partner, Mikołajczyk. The house we lived in belonged to the *boss* and still belongs to him today. He had a *saloon* and a grocery store there, and we lived on the second floor, [with an] entrance from First Avenue.

I had a whole two weeks of vacation because immediately after our arrival, my father found work in St. Martins — Franklin at that time —

and came for me on the Fourth of July, and took me with him because he found work for me with a *farmer* for five dollars and *board* a month. That was almost the only vacation I had in my whole life because from that time on, it was, "Work, fellow, because you have been fooling around long enough."

I served there for two months, and during that time my father rented a house from a *farmer* close to Franklin. It was an old *log house* because the *farmer* lived in a new one. [My father] brought my mother and two younger sisters there. I came home, too, and worked there for the *farmers*, and on Sundays I pumped the organ in the St. Martins Church, and from this you can see that I wasn't idle.

That *farmer* whose place I lived on was an old boneheaded Dutchman, Fred Jansen, and he didn't speak any other language well. I learned to speak Dutch pretty well there, but I've almost completely forgotten it, because that was more than sixty years ago, but I can still sing one song well. Almost everybody there wore wooden clogs, including me, and even today if I took a nip I would dance a jig in them — not dry, though, because nobody does something for free. I still keep a pair for a souvenir, and my granddaughter, Cecylia Drożniakiewicz, won first prize in them at the high school on Eighth Avenue and Lapham Street. [...]

We didn't live long with that *farmer* because my father bought a forty-acre *farm* a little farther out, on the south side of Muskego Lake. It was one big lake, not like now when it is divided into parts — Muskego Center, Muskego Bay, and so on — only one big one, and it went as far as Wind Lake. Our field went right up to the lake. That's where we took our cattle to drink. In winter I went fishing there, because in summer I didn't have time, since I worked every day for the *farmers* and on Sunday at the organ, and I didn't have a boat. But when winter came, I went very often, because my father made me a little sled and I put our basin for washing linens on it, and off to fishing.

I remember once, it was a Thursday and it was a foggy day when I went and made some twenty holes. Everyone could make as many as he wanted. The first fish I caught was a small perch, so I put it on a long line and put it down in the water but only some three feet, and it was riding around there as if on a carousel. Not long after, a big pike arrived and swallowed it. As I was pulling it out, it turned out that the hole was too small, and meanwhile a couple of fishermen came up. One says in German, "Let him go," and I made a bigger hole. Then he grabbed the line himself, and he was an old hand, for fishing was his profession, and he pulled very slowly until the head appeared in the hole. Then he jerked it and the pike was lying on the ice. It was a nice specimen, because it weighed more than eight pounds. That day I caught a full basin of different kinds, pike, perch, crucian carp, and *bullheads*, and the next day my father got up at four and took them to Milwaukee and sold them well. From the small fry Mother made us a *sweet dinner* and there were still some left for supper.

And we were doing well, because there was a lot of work, if not for the *farmers* then at home, since we already had a horse, three cows, pigs, geese, and chickens. If Father had lived longer, we might still live there today, but misfortune willed that Father fell sick with dropsy and did not recover, but died, and so we lost a good father and a resourceful master of the house. [...]

When [Father] got very weak, my brother Paweł went to town for our brothers and they were all there when he died. I went with a *farmer* — our neighbor, Sym — and Fred Jansen, whose place we had lived at, to fetch the priest at two o'clock at night. He told me what to say and I ran across the Bosch *farm shortcut*. When I got to the rectory and knocked, the priest asked [in German], "Who is there?" I say [in German], "Matas (Maciej), Paul's son. Father is very sick"; and he was "very glad to go." Nobody there called my father anything but Paul. He came out quickly and went right away to the church for the holy sacrament, and when the *farmer* arrived [with his wagon], the priest was already waiting for him. The priest found my father still in his right mind, and he was able to confess and receive the holy sacrament. When the same *farmer* took the priest back, he said to the *farmer* [in German], "Fred, I don't think Paul is so very weak yet" — the *farmer* told us later. When they came to the rectory, the priest got down off the wagon — and this was a big *farmer's* wagon with a high seat — and said [in German], "Fred, wait a little." And he went to the cellar and brought [back] a bottle of wine and said [in German], "Take this for Paul. Perhaps it will make him stronger." When the *farmer* came back, my father was dead. He died on November 27, 1870, and he was born in 1815. Mother was younger than Father, and she died when she was eighty-two years old.

When my older brothers went to tell the priest about it, he was surprised because he didn't think Father was that weak yet. He told them when the funeral would be. Then he went to the school. He announced

who had died and told the children to be so good as to tell their parents to
come to the funeral if they could. And since there wasn't a lot of work at
that time, almost everybody came and it was a very big funeral. All the
sons carried Father, so that later the *farmers* said it was perhaps the first
such funeral in their parish, where the sons could perform such a service
for their father. I went to Milwaukee for a coffin, and the same farmer who
went to bring the priest carried the body to the church, and on the same
wagon. The priest celebrated the Holy Mass, gave a eulogy, and came
to the cemetery of his own free will. Later, when my older brothers went
to pay him, he said, "It won't cost you anything; only be good to your two
little sisters" — since they attended his school and he knew them — "because this lad Matas can already support himself."

That same priest would change his clothes right after the Holy Mass
and work in his garden, but all his tools had long *handles* because he was
a very big man. He once bought a new station of the cross for the
church. The *farmers* were not pleased, and they reproached him, saying
they would have made it for him if he had only asked. He answered
them politely, "And what am I to do with my money? My old housekeeper and I don't need much." He also had an old granny, his relative,
and the *farmers* said that he could at least send money to his parents in
the old country. They lived in Trier near the French border. "My parents
are not poor," [he replied.] "They have enough to eat, and anyway the
poorer a man is, the happier. My parents didn't send me to become a
priest in order to make thousands, but to serve God and His people, and
I do it with my conscience clear." That's how it was in those days in
Franklin with that priest Beringer or Geringer, I don't remember any
more exactly.

And so it was the end of our *farm*, because there was no one to run
it. I was too young, and secondly, there were still debts to pay off, so there
was nothing to do but sell it. So my brother Michał, to whom it was
signed over because he put the most money into it, exchanged it for a city
property, number 400 Maple Street. He lived there until his death, and
took in Mother and two of our sisters, because he was obligated to take
care of Mother until her death, and of our sisters until they could
manage by themselves, which he fulfilled honestly and gladly. My sisters
finished school there — the older, Paulina, at that little old church at
Grove and Mineral Streets [the first St. Stanislaus Church] and the
younger, Ewa, in the new one at Grove and Mitchell. I [also] lived there,

but as the priest said, "That lad will take care of himself." I worked [in Milwaukee], but not for long, because some partners persuaded me, and four of us went to Michigan. We wanted to go to Mackinaw, but because there was too big a storm, the ship couldn't enter the port and took us to Port Huron. [The ship] wanted to take us back, but we stayed there, that is, I, my brother Paweł, Walenty Kańdziora, and Andrzej Szołowicz.

[...] At last we came to Bay City [Michigan]. We got a job there, and we met some acquaintances from our village, Izabela. It was the cook, Stanisław Śmiałek, and Józef Welter, the servant, because the Koczo-rowskis went bankrupt, so they didn't need such freeloaders, so [Stanisław and Józef] went to America, to Bay City, and there they worked in a sawmill. We lodged with them by twos. At that time there were five or six families and several *farmers*, Polish ones. This was 1871. And today there are some two or three Polish churches, one apparently at Bridgeport. It was quite a distance from town, way in the corner of Bay. At that time there was already one big new sawmill there. In my time, a wide river cut through Bay City, and the other side of the river was called Wenona, and a long bridge ran [across] and the crossing cost three cents. I worked in Bay City the whole summer and almost until Christmas in a salt works. [...]

By the time I left for Milwaukee I had $150.00, two new suits, and a silver watch worth $15. I bought a ticket all the way to Milwaukee and it cost $8.25. In Owosso I had to change cars and wait three hours until the train from Detroit arrived and took me to Grand Haven and from there by boat to Milwaukee. I didn't stay there for long, and during that time I bought a ticket [to America] for Uncle Paweł Mulka from Białośliwie, and then I went to Chicago.

It was just after the Great Fire. I worked there until almost fall and went to Michigan again, but this time to Kalamazoo, where they were building a new railway, and Lansing because they were starting to build a new capitol there. The foundation was already finished. There, I voted for the first time in my life, and that was for president in 1872, for Greeley, but Grant was elected in the first round. I was not yet of age, only twenty, but an old Irishman I worked with voted first, and he pushed me out [in front of him] and said, "*This is mine sonny, Math. McCarty*," and the matter was closed. From that time on I have never missed any elections, always a Democrat for president; for smaller offices I always vote for the proper people, and always for Poles, although they are all of the same kind, thieves, whether Democrat or Republican, and everyone steals as much as he can, and Socialists, those braggarts, the most.

When I came back to Milwaukee there was only a week until Christmas. But I didn't stay long here because the wind was not yet out of my noggin and I still wanted to taste more misery, which also came not long after, because I went again to Muskegon, Michigan. I worked in a mill there the whole summer, and I had it good there, because in the place where I dined everybody liked me, including the proprietress, and most of all the girls, since I wouldn't go anywhere in the evenings, but just helped the girls, and then I played with them, and I liked it and they did, too. When that job in the mill was over at the end of November, this curious Maciek (Matt) wanted, by all means, to see what kind of life [lumberjacks] led in the forest, and I quickly found out — almost too quickly. And let that kind of life go to the devils, if there are any, since some say there are none but I don't know. [...]

I made up my mind that it was enough of such foolishness, and when I came [back] to Milwaukee I didn't leave again without good reason. I set about learning carpentry at John Fellens's. [...] It was the pure truth that he was a friend of the Poles and employed many Poles because he always had a lot of work and big state constructions, and he built churches. He belonged to Holy Trinity Church, and he came from Germany, from Trier, somewhere near the French border. He never said "you Polack" to anybody at all. The late Rakowski would sometimes talk back; then he [would say], "You always have to know better!" but not "Polack."

When I began to work for him — and I worked many years — my brother Piotr was already working for him, and he was building St. Anthony's Church at Mitchell and Fourth Avenue. Not long before, he bought our old church [the first St. Stanislaus Church] at Grove and Mineral Streets and turned it into a [work]*shop*. The frames for St. Anthony's Church were made there. [...] Soon after, he built a church for the Capuchins. Six of us Poles worked there: I, my brother Piotr, Aleksander Sawicki, Andrzej Rakowski (the father of the pharmacist, Stanisław), and two other Poles.

He also built a Capuchin church beyond Calvary cemetery, and you had to hoof it everywhere, because the streetcars only went as far as Seventh and Elizabeth Street, today's National Avenue. Then he sent me four miles past Schleisingerville [now Slinger]. He was building a rectory there, and then a church for a German parish. Father Weiss was there and he was a good priest, somewhat advanced in years. He would take us to a *saloon* every Saturday night, and he bought cigars, vodka, and beer, but again, not enough for us to get drunk. He would sit with us, himself, and drink until eleven, and then he would say, "Now I must go home. You can stay here a while," and he would tell the *saloon* keeper to give us more if we wanted to drink. But [then, in German], "Mind, you all come tomorrow to church." And I would say [in German], "Yes, Father Weiss, we will all come." And he liked me, although he always quarreled with me. And so, he would blow up at me [...]: "You city loafer! It's good that this job will soon be over, because you would corrupt all the boy and girls here, especially the girls."

And on Sunday we went, not quite to the church, but near the church. He knew us very well and he knew where we were, so before he went to the pulpit, he came out of the sacristy and chased us into church. "You'd better get into church," [he said, in German]. But don't think that a little *farmers'* church in the olden days was as big as St. Josaphat's Church is today. No, it was a little tiny building. He could see everyone there and especially us [hedonists], because he always kept us in sight. When he came to us on Monday morning after the Holy Mass, once again Matas got it on the nose. I fibbed that we just went out to get some fresh air. "Don't lie to me, you gypsy," he says. "I didn't see you there at all, because you weren't there at all."

[...] Oh yes, I had a great time there, not like in the Michigan forest. There was plenty to eat and drink and it was a good job. There were good boys there and even better girls. You could live and not die there. The old and the young there liked me very much, because I was polite to everybody. I always tipped my hat to an older person and [said] "Good day" or "Good evening." I dined in the *saloon*, and on the second floor there was a dance hall. There was always a ball on the first Saturday [of the month], and I would call the quadrille, and I could do it well because I learned it from a book. The boys and girls liked me because of this, and told me to my face that they don't like city boys, because they are too fancy, but "you are not like that," because I was always good buddies with them. "*Hallo, boys. Hallo, girls! How do you do?*" [I would say]. And right away, I would wink at the girls, and they likewise at me. From this, I found favor with them, because I knew how to handle them. Those *saloon* keepers liked me a lot, and especially the missus, because I often did things for her and was eager and would say, "Let me do this for Auntie," so that when I left, she said, "I thought you would be my son-in-law, because I like you, since you are not a drunk or a troublemaker. I would like to have such a son-in-law."

And she had two pretty little fillies, good hardworking girls, but so what, when they were Germans — although Catholics. They didn't know that I was a Pole, because I spoke German as well as they did, but I was a Pole and furthermore a Poznań man, so I leaned toward my own. At that time, however, I don't know what might have happened, because after my departure from there I missed those people very much, and especially the older daughter, Barbara. I preferred her to the younger, Katie.

Those people liked me as their own son. I felt at home there, too, and I played with the girls as with my sisters, only when I stole a *kiss* from one, it was nicer than from a sister. But I wasn't a saint, either, just a bungler like all the rest, and I don't know what might have happened, whether blood is thicker than water, because those people were not those vengeful Prussians, but from Belgium. But by a strange coincidence, I came across a still prettier gal, and it was in a strange way, because it was at geese tending. Perhaps you will think again that I am bragging. *Oh no, that's a fact*, as will be demonstrated right away. Because when we finished our job there, our *boss* took us right away to the train at West Bend and from there to Oshkosh. He had a big *contract* there, four miles outside of Oshkosh. A home for the mentally ill. When we finished that job, I went home to my brother's. Before that, my brother had bought eight geese to fatten and the devils did not want to eat, because they were almost all ganders, so they just stood and gaggled. And my sister-in-law complained to Mother that the geese wouldn't eat, but my mother said, "No, they will eat with pleasure. You will just buy me bran and rapeseed meal and I have ashes here." And she made dumplings and fed them [to the geese] whether they wanted them or not, with water for washing it down. So in three weeks, those geese were so fat that they couldn't walk.

On the second day after my arrival, Mother says, "My boy, you could drive these geese to the water, to swim." There was a little pond on Maple Street just past First Avenue, going north. I drove them there and broke the ice with a stick, because the ice was already formed but still thin, and they swam, and then, to make matters worse, I had to carry them home wet, because they couldn't walk anymore. Every couple of steps they would sit, and they were heavy gray hogs, and wet to boot.

While I was tending them, two women passed by. I knew one of them. It was Magdalena Szweda, a cook in the servants' quarters in Izabela, and at that time already the wife of Michał Mazur, half-brother of the young girl who walked with her. [The girl] was shapely, like in a painting, the scamp, and she was an only daughter, Ewa Kołodziejska. I talked with them a good while and Mrs. Mazur invited me to visit them and said, "He who flatters the mother will kiss the daughter." This didn't have to be repeated twice, because I was all for it, and flattering mothers was my craft, although I didn't study it as long as carpentry, but I was able to do it better, like a lawyer. So I didn't wait long, but ran right over there that evening, as if I'd been touched with a hot iron.

And it was true, what Mrs. Mazur said, because after that I kissed the daughter forever until death, because we got to know each other the same evening, since they lived together in the same house [...]. From that time on, I was there so often that we got to know each other very well and fell in love, and no one could chase me away from there anymore, not even with *police dogs*. I soon forgot about those other [girls], too, because with this one I could speak Polish. Although I spoke German well, it is always nicer to speak one's own language than a foreign one. [...] When my Ewunia (Evie) and I came to a good understanding, I didn't look at others anymore and didn't eye any others, and we were faithful to each other, and we went together like siblings, only this siblinghood was much nicer, and so we went together for almost three years. In 1875 I worked in St. Francis at the Seminary, where they learned to be priests, and in the late fall our *boss* sent us again, my brother and me, to Madison.

He had a big house to build there where they learn to be thieves — I should have said lawyers and teachers. We put in the foundation and flooring there, and then back to Milwaukee. At the beginning of 1876 [Ewa and I] asked the banns, and on January 18 we got married in St. Stanislaus Church. There was a Capuchin, Father Kralczyński. We had to go to him for examination, like in the old country, and we did so willingly, which pleased him a lot. He was very satisfied with us, because he praised us from the pulpit at the last banns and said we were excellent in religion, while the truth was that I sometimes made an error, for what did I remember from the catechism, since I only had nonsense in my head, but my gal spoke as if from a book. We were engaged almost two years before we got married, not like it is today: today they meet, tomorrow they ride to Waukegon and get married, and after a month, divorce,

Revoir! And they say that people are wiser now and have made a lot of progress. [...]

We only lived in Milwaukee for two months, and in March I went again with my brother Piotr to Madison, to the same job. I was there two weeks, and I rented a little house from a bricklayer who worked with us. It was a good little old house with a big garden and only two blocks from the job. Then my sweetheart joined me and that's when we had our honeymoon, just like nowadays when they go away to another city. Soon those old workers who worked on the Seminary came — Sawicki, Rakowski, and one German, Christ Baum. We had all worked before in Oshkosh, so we knew each other well — only I had to lodge them because they didn't want to go anywhere else. Then Wojciech Młynarski came. We knew each other way back from Chicago, but we couldn't take him in because there was no room. We were sorry that he had to go somewhere else, to strangers.

There my Ewunia at once set herself to taking care of that little garden. And my job was to go every evening to the butcher and the grocer to order things, and the next day they would deliver. There was a fashion there that nobody carried things but everything was delivered. Once I forgot yeast but the grocer brought it right away because my whirlwind of a young housewife baked her own bread, and what good bread! And she kept after my brother and Christ to help her dig the garden. Christ was a *farmer* and a good boy, and later a good friend. He lived seven miles out of town on Kilbourn Road. We often visited him there later. We lived there until the job was finished, and my little pearl worked the entire summer long in that garden. And as the *farmers* say, she had a *good crop* because the soil was rested and well manured, so much so that the neighbor ladies marveled and said, *"That young lady is a hard worker."* (They were just blockheaded Irish women who doubtless never held a spade in their hands and didn't know anything but how to blabber.) And the main thing was that [Ewa] was never *late* with either dinner or supper, but it was always "Be seated" at the table, which everyone marveled at, and they all gave her a lot of *credit*, because they didn't know how she could do it when they always saw her in the garden. [...]

When I asked her how she did it, she said, "As long as I have a good clock, there's nothing to it, because for everything, time has to be calculated."

We went to a German Catholic church there, and [at this church] there was a different custom from our Polish churches. I rented two seats and wanted [them] somewhere at the back, but what can you do when there were none to rent except in the front, where it was almost empty, even though they went for $1.50 in the back and for $1.25 in the front. That was because people liked to come late and fly out fast. The sacristan led us all the way to the *front*, just behind the Sisters. Only a good old woman sat there, along with the two of us. We never saw any people. When we came in, nobody was there yet, and when we left, the church was empty, too, except for the Sisters and our neighbor, the good old woman.

At that time only one Polish family lived [in the area], from Połajewo, Duchy of Poznań, where the late Ernest Krenc and Jan Jęśko came from. They were very good people, already elderly. They had two daughters already married, but they lived in Janesville, and one son. He was a *bartender* and later had his own *saloon* called Mike Nomen Blue Front Restaurant, although his real name was Michał Nowak. We got to know them and went to see them every Sunday and sometimes every day in the evening when time permitted. They were very tough Polish people. They couldn't speak a word of German. We liked to visit them because we could speak Polish. They couldn't read or write, but they could talk as if from a book and always had a lot to say, and we were happy to listen.

Our first son, Józef, was born there, in 1876, the fifth of October, but I had a lot of trouble with him [that is, with his birth], for while a good master of the house takes care of everything ahead of time, we dummies waited until the last minute. Then what, then fly, Maciek, to Mrs. Nowak, and it was a long way and already past midnight and I was beating it at top speed, because she [Ewa] was left there alone and when I told Mrs. Nowak, she said: "My boy, what have you two done? This is no joke!" and quickly put on a dress and ran with me to a certain old lady. When I told her, she quickly got dressed and hobbled along with me as fast as she could.

And when she got there and saw [Ewa], she said, "It's high time," and at five in the morning there was a nine-pound son. Only then did I find out what honeymoons mean, a sick wife and four boarders, and I didn't know beans about cooking, and no help from anywhere. To be sure, a couple of Irish women came, but only to get in the way because they did nothing but buzz, over and over, *"feel sorry,"* but didn't look at the dishes, and there was quite a pile to be washed. If they had been

Polish women, one of them would have put on an apron right away and washed them, instead of me, but this way I had to struggle with them as best I could. I rinsed them a bit and the coffee mugs not at all. I just poured coffee into a mug until it overflowed into a saucer and it was all okay. [...] For three days I had to struggle alone, until Mrs. Nowak found a housekeeper.

She was a young divorcée. She was with us six weeks and she kept house well. My gal liked her because she was very thrifty and didn't waste anything. Right after the birth, I wrote and my mother-in-law came with my brother-in-law, Jan Kołodziejski, because my wife had one full brother, but instead of helping me, Mrs. Mother got sick herself, and very much so. [...]

When that job was over we came to Milwaukee and remained there for good. We stayed at my brother Michał's, 400 Maple Street. We lived there several years until we bought ourselves a small property at number 758 Garden Street, and we lived there many years. Almost all our children were born there, and several on Maple Street, all of them [baptized by] the late Father Gulski in St. Stanislaus Church. He was a very good preacher; he liked us very much and we [liked] him as well. I enlarged and restored that little house; then we sold the place, because it was too small a property for my wife. We bought two lots on First Avenue past the Northwestern railway tracks.

There I built a big *flat* and a big pigsty, and there my wife really extended herself and showed what she could do. She had a whole farmstead there, that is, chickens, geese, ducks, pigeons, a cow, and pigs. We also had a horse, because I was already contracting then, and she [Ewa] took care of everything by herself, and very skillfully. She even took care of the horse by herself, except for cleaning, and almost always when I came home, the horse already had something in the trough. She filled him up so much that whatever she put in, he gobbled up, and every time she came to the pigsty, he would address her. The last cow we had was a purebred, and she had a calf. It was a heifer, and it was growing, and it was already several months old and healthy, but it died suddenly — we don't know of what.

That saddened my housewife very much, so I had to console her that there must be an end to everything, and it was a very nice, cheerful little calf. When my housewife went outside, it ran up to her, since it was already walking around on the grass.

We always killed quite a lot of ducks for the winter, some ten geese, and a piglet. One time, the late Jan Boncel, the butcher, came and slaughtered three piglets. When we didn't have our own we would buy them. Another time, on Garden Street, [Ewa] bought four slaughtered sheep from Emil Keller. All of this was salted and smoked. And when summer came and everything was expensive, we had our own, that is, hams, sausages, fatback, goose fat for bread, and fat for cooking and frying, and it tasted ten times better than if it had been bought. Such a housewife was my wife, and a cook — if not the best in the whole world, then for sure in all of America, because her mother had worked twelve years for the master's cook, so she taught her everything well.

And she was a good mother, even too good, because she loved the children too much and gave them too much freedom, and when she couldn't manage them, then [she would say] to me: "I don't know what kind of father you are; you don't take any care of them." When I took care of them, but in a father's way, then she [was] again after me: "I will devour them. Devour — it's enough to tell you something and you don't know when to stop." "But woman, am I going to coddle them like you?" Because when she was beating [them] they were screaming until it rang in your ears but when I whacked [them], even if they wanted to [scream], they couldn't.

From this it sometimes came to quarrels, but not for long, because when I saw that she was pouting, I [would say]: "Mama, are you angry?" (That's how we addressed each other when the children began to say "mama" and "daddy" and that's how we kept doing it, but before, it was Maciek and Ewka [Evie].) Are we going to be angry with each other over these silly kids — after all we cannot be angry forever — so sooner or later [one of us would say], "Give me a kiss."

"First you'll tear off a person's head, and then you want to put it back on, that's the kind of fellow you are," [she would say]. But she would give [me a kiss] and again there was the best possible harmony. [...]

We did well for ourselves, and we loved and respected each other very much. One didn't hide anything from the other, and we always knew what the other one was doing. When I wanted to go somewhere, I would tell her:

"Mama, I'm going here and here."

"Then go, but don't play long and come back soon, and perhaps you would like a couple of cents."

And even though I had [money], I would say, "Oh, a couple of cents? A couple of dollars!"

"Not a couple of dollars. Just take a dollar, but don't squander it, and bring it back."

"And what use is it to me, if I have to bring it back? Then you'd better keep it for yourself."

"No, take it, just in case. I know you won't squander it, but I don't want you to find yourself without money, either."

And truly, at that time you could do more with a dollar than today with five *bucks*. She wouldn't buy anything without my knowledge, and she always asked my advice about it. When the children sometimes wanted her to buy them something, [she would say], "Well, children, I have to ask Daddy first. I can't do it myself because Daddy might be angry. Because Daddy is working for us, and so he is the *boss*." That's what kind of married couple we were. My wife's one fault was that she sided too much with the children, because when I said something, then she [would say]: "Yes, and you are better!" And that spoiled the children. But who doesn't have any faults? I wasn't a saint either, because everyone has something. I was not a drunk but I didn't refuse [a drink] either, nor a liar, nor a card shark, although I liked to play cards but never for money or in a *saloon*, only in a private house, with friends, for fun.

Our children were not bad, but neither were they the best. Some have better, but others ten times worse. With ours we didn't have great embarrassment, that is, with the boys, because they were not drunks or loafers, but only a little dull in their studies. When they finished primary school, they were supposed to go on for higher learning, but they preferred to go to work, and you know that obligatory study is worth nothing. We didn't object much because we thought that when they had enough of work they would go to school. But far from it, because then there was nothing of study nor much of work, since when they could have helped us, Zygfryd and Ignacy joined the army. In the army they performed well and brought back good papers: Zygfryd, "*Excellent,*" and Ignacy, "*Very good,*" because Ignacy was more careless than Zygfryd.

Both served in the mountain artillery. They were in Cuba for two years, and after they got out, they were thinking about themselves. And the girls, although they worked — well, what could a girl earn then? Not even enough for her own needs. Not like today, when a good girl can earn more than many a boy.

And so we didn't have much help from our children, but we were glad that we didn't have to subsidize them as many parents had to, and even today have to. We didn't have to do that, and we were glad. We gave them as much help as we could, and we never complained about them, and they never went to sleep hungry, and we always had something to eat and to wear. My son Józef, number one, the one who was born in Madison, he helped me the most, because he worked with me when I began to contract on my own, naturally not for nothing. Sons want *pay*, which they rightly deserve. Tadeusz, the youngest, the *baby* — we had nothing out of him, only costs, because he kept going to school the longest and got the most education. But so what, when he doesn't use it? Whatever comes in, goes out, so he doesn't have anything for a rainy day. Although he doesn't drink or smoke, his pockets are empty, because if he has a couple of dollars, they burn a hole in his pocket, and right away it's to New York or to California or to Canada, and everything *high-tone*. But let him run his affairs as to his wishes, because he got out from under my hoof a long time ago, since he is over thirty, so he is old enough and should know what he is doing. He doesn't listen to his old father anyway, so let it be this way, because it's not my worry.

But we soon had much bigger trouble, because a great misfortune visited us — but who is without it? On December 1, 1902, we had a big fire, and almost everything burned. The pigsty completely — as Marcin Czerwiński, who was the agent of the [insurance] policy, said, "*Clean sweep.*" We got the cow and pigs out, but everything else went up in smoke, that is, the horse, chickens, and pigeons, and I had my carpentry shop on the second floor, so all the carpentry tools and a lot of wood and hay were burned, and it was insured only for six hundred [dollars], which we received, but the loss was some two thousand.

And the house burned so fiercely that we had to run away from it, and what we carried out of it was stolen by thieves, because there were neither policemen nor fire hoses. When the firemen came from town the whole house was already on fire, and the loss was estimated at eighteen hundred [dollars] but we only had insurance for fifteen hundred, which we received in full. I had to renovate the whole house and make it smaller, because the back part was completely burned down, since the fire started in the pigsty, and we had to look for a different place to live. So we rented a small house on the northeast corner of Garden and Grant Streets. We lived there two months, and during this time we bought a small property from Józef Bronikowski, 946 Chicago Avenue, now 2244 South Chase Avenue, which I renovated and enlarged. We lived here for many years because my "mama" liked to go to church and from here it was very close [to St. Josaphat]. [My son] Józef and [daughter] Frania Śliżewska lived in the house [on First Avenue] that I renovated after the fire.

But after that fire, something was always wrong. My wife came down with typhoid once, and it was so bad that all her hair fell out and she had to wear a wig. And when she recovered from that misery and her hair began to grow back, it was as long as today's ladies,' who have their beautiful hair cut even with their ears — I really don't know what for; maybe they copied it from my "mama" — but she didn't do it on purpose, only because she had to.

About a year later, she fell sick again and did not recover this time, but died on the twentieth of August, 1918, at two in the morning. I want to die right here, and now I am waiting for my turn, since I didn't take any other [wife] on my shoulders — and this is because I love my children and the children respect me, and they are good to me. And if I had taken some woman, then, well, fine, I would have a wife, but the question is, what kind? For sure, not the kind my gal was. And the children wouldn't have a mother anyway, and if she were a scold, then they might neglect their father and there would be a big misunderstanding. This way, at least I have good children, and they like their old father, and we have peace and harmony, and I don't need to fear that I will have to go to the *poor farm*.

Shortly after the funeral I brought my daughter Frania in, and she keeps house for me to this day. She doesn't pay me *rent*, but instead she feeds me and does the wash and keeps house for me. She is already a widow because her husband, Stanisław Śliżewski, died the ninth of February, 1925. He was a boilermaker. He worked in the Milwaukee West shops [of the Chicago, Milwaukee & St. Paul Railway]. He hurt himself there and was operated on in the hospital and died. He was a good and hardworking man. [...]

My daughter runs the house with her children and doesn't suffer from poverty because she has good kids — hardworking. They give her everything they earn, and they have their own bankbooks. The oldest, Dawid, is a bit tightfisted, but that is ten times better than if [he] were a spendthrift. He makes good money because he is a machinist and a very diligent worker, so he is always working, and he is thinking of getting married soon. He already has his chosen one, his little pearl, and it is high time, too, because he's a big fellow, already thirty. The second was Aleksander. He died when he was a year and a half old. The third is daughter Elżbieta, twenty-five years old. She will probably never marry, because she is afraid of boys. She is a very quiet, hardworking girl, she doesn't run around to *dances*, but goes to school every evening and studies home economics, that is, how to sew, to cook, and many other things, such as how to make flowers, et cetera, and the rest of the time she helps her mother at home. And when she bakes a *cake*, it even invites itself to be tasted. The fourth is Alicja, twenty-one. She is already engaged to Harry Prokop. She is a know-it-all. She is a *clerk* at Frank Krens's, electrician, on Mitchell Street, and when she is the cook in the kitchen, then you can lick your chops and be sure that there will be a *number one meal*, and she is a good, gay, alert girl.

The fifth is Estera, nineteen years old. If she gets a quiet husband, he will have a good housewife, because she is a very hardworking girl, not a lazy bones, *oh no, no siree!* But if she gets one who won't allow himself to be pushed around, then there will be quarrels, because she doesn't give in to anybody. I have to quarrel the most with her, because if I [say] one word, then she [says] ten, and everything comes out for her as if she had it written in a book, like a special lawyer. But on the other hand, work burns in her fingernails. She is a very good-natured girl, because just as she is quick to argue, she is still quicker to make up. She likes me very much, nearly most of all.

The sixth and the last is my gal, Dorota (Dorothy), ten years old, because she is my goddaughter. When her father died, her mother said: "Dorotka (Dot), now you will not have Daddy." Then she: "I don't care. Grandpa will be my daddy." And that little whippersnapper was right, because I pamper her more than her daddy, and I take care of her like the apple of my eye. Now she washes my back every Saturday, for which she gets *pay*, always five cents, and on Sunday when she comes from church, also five cents. And when she was little and was going to give me a kiss, she would say, "Grandpa scratches," and apparently it was true, because I gave her [a kiss] from my sincere heart and for sure it scratched her.

I have the most trouble with her, because, for the living God, I cannot keep up with her in talking, since when I say something to her in Polish, she replies in English. It happened once that she went outside and it was winter and she didn't close the door, but left it ajar, and the door opened again, so I went out and said: "Dorotka, when you go out, please be so good as to close the door behind you, because now is not the season for the door to be open." Then she closed it, but so hard that all four panes rattled in it, because they were glass, so that my daughter, her mother, came out and said, "What's going on, Dorotka?"

And she [mixing Polish and English]: "Grandpa *scolds*."

"Whom?"

"Me."

"And for what?"

"When I *door open* then I again have to *close* it."

"Well, but not so hard, after all."

"When I *close* it slowly, then it again *open*."

Such is today's Polish speech in children, and it's no better with many older people, and soon it will be still worse. And whose fault is this? Some blame others and nobody wants to be at fault, but in fairness we are all a bit guilty. But again, not so much as some think, because here in America every nationality distorts its language, but the Poles for sure the most, because many distort it on purpose and so much that it is unpleasant to hear.

Selected Bibliography

Borun, Thaddeus, ed. *We, the Milwaukee Poles*. Milwaukee: Nowiny Publishing Co., 1946.

Bukowczyk, John J. *A History of the Polish Americans*. New Brunswick, NJ: Transaction Publishers, 2008.

Galush, William J. *For More than Bread: Community and Identity in American Polonia, 1880–1940*. Boulder: East European Monographs, 2006.

Goc, Michael J. *Native Realm: The Polish-American Community of Portage County, 1857–1992*. Stevens Point: Worzalla Publishing, 1992.

Kenny, Judith. "Polish Routes to Americanization: House Form and Landscape on Milwaukee's Polish South Side." In *Wisconsin Land and Life*, Robert C. Ostergren and Thomas R. Vale, ed. Madison: The University of Wisconsin Press, 1997.

Kolinski, Dennis L. "Shrines and Crosses in Rural Central Wisconsin." In *Wisconsin Folklore*. James P. Leary, ed. Madison: The University of Wisconsin Press, 1998.

Kriehn, Ruth. *The Fisherfolk of Jones Island*. Milwaukee: Milwaukee County Historical Society, 1992.

Kruszka, Wacław. *A History of the Poles in America to 1908*. 4 vols. James S. Pula, ed. Washington, DC: The Catholic University of America Press, 1993–2001.

Kuzniewski, Anthony J. *Faith and Fatherland: The Polish Church War in Wisconsin, 1896–1918*. Notre Dame: University of Notre Dame Press, 1980.

Maass, Christel T. *Illuminating the Particular: Photographs of Milwaukee's Polish South Side*. Madison: Wisconsin Historical Society Press, 2003.

Pease, Neal. "The Kosciuszko Reds, 1909–1919: Kings of the Milwaukee Sandlots." *Polish American Studies* LXI.1 (2004): 11–26.

Pienkos, Donald. "Politics, Religion, and Change in Polish Milwaukee, 1900–1930." *Wisconsin Magazine of History* 61.3 (1977/78): 178–209.

Pula, James S. et al, eds. *The Polish American Encyclopedia*. Jefferson, NC: McFarland & Co., Inc.

———. *Polish Americans: An Ethnic Community*. New York: Twayne Publishers, 1995.

Zeitlin, Richard H. "White Eagles in the North Woods: Polish Immigration to Rural Wisconsin, 1857–1900." *The Polish Review* XXV.1 (1980): 69–92.

INDEX